The Agile Manager's Guide To

DELEGATING
WORK

The Agile Manager's Guide To

DELEGATING WORK

By Joseph T. Straub

Velocity Business Publishing
Bristol, Vermont USA

Copyright © 1998 by Joseph T. Straub
All Rights Reserved
Printed in the United States of America
Library of Congress Catalog Card Number 97-81356
ISBN 1-58099-009-6
Design by Andrea Gray
Title page illustration by Elayne Sears

If you'd like additional copies of this book or a catalog of books in the Agile Manager Series™, please get in touch with us.

- **Write us at:**
Velocity Business Publishing, Inc.
15 Main Street
Bristol, VT 05443 USA

- **Call us at:**
1-888-805-8600 in North America (toll-free)
1-802-453-6669 from all other countries

- **Fax us at:**
1-802-453-2164

- **E-mail us at:**
info@agilemanager.com

- **Visit our Web site at:**
www.agilemanager.com

The Web site contains much of interest to business people—tips and techniques, business news, links to valuable sites, and electronic versions of titles in the Agile Manager Series.

Call or write for a free, time-saving "extra-fast" edition of this book—or visit www.agilemanager.com.

For Pat and Stacey

Contents

Introduction: Delegation Ain't Natural 9

1. Delegate to Get Ahead 15

2. Delegate the Right Jobs 26

3. The Basics of Successful Delegation 33

4. Communicate the Assignment 45

5. Deal with Resistance 57

6. Oversee the Job 69

7. Handle a Non-Delegating Boss 83

Appendix: Internet Resources 91

Index 93

Other Books in the Agile Manager Series™:

Giving Great Presentations
Understanding Financial Statements
Motivating People
Making Effective Decisions
Leadership
Goal-Setting and Achievement
Great Customer Service
Customer-Focused Selling
Cutting Costs
Effective Performance Appraisals
Writing to Get Action
Hiring Excellence
Building and Leading Teams
Getting Organized

Delegation Ain't Natural

So you're uncomfortable about delegating. Who isn't? Fortunately, you're also savvy enough to do something about it. If you weren't, you wouldn't be reading this book!

Few people enjoy handing down authority, for reasons we'll look at soon. In fact, there's probably no such thing as a "natural delegator." Delegation isn't something that comes naturally, no matter how agile a manager is.

Delegation: It's No Piece of Cake—for Anyone

Consider the approach this inept manager takes to delegating work:

> *Inept Manager:* "Marilyn, I'd like you to . . ."
> *Worker:* "Fred. My name's not Marilyn; it's Fred."
> *Inept Manager:* "Whatever. I'd like you to put this monthly production report together, starting today."
> *Worker:* "In the words of that old Johnny Paycheck song, 'Take this job and . . .'"

Now let's look at how an agile manager does it:

Agile Manager: "Helen, I'd like you to . . ."

Worker (bursting into tears, punctuated by wracking sobs): "Good Lord, not another 'little job'! I'm about to have a nervous breakdown because of the workload I have now!"

Agile Manager: "I understand your misgivings, Helen, but please hear me out. I'd like you to take over publishing our department's monthly production report. It will give you an opportunity to make new contacts in several departments and broaden your decision-making and human relations skills. We agreed that those were areas that needed improvement when we went over your career-development plan last month. In addition, taking charge of this report should enhance your promotability. Let's set up a meeting tomorrow to go over the details. I'm confident you'll do your best."

Worker (regaining her composure and smiling brightly): "I'm suddenly reminded of the words to a country song by Johnny Paycheck. They go like this . . ."

In other words, delegation is no piece of cake, even for the most able managers. Sometimes it can be a can of worms. But let's look closer.

Delegation: Some Hate It, the Rest Loathe It

Many managers approach delegation with the same enthusiasm they'd feel when faced with having a root canal done by a blacksmith. That's not surprising, really, because they might be:

1. **Perfectionists.** Is there a manager alive who hasn't said, at one time or another, "If you want something done right, do it yourself"? It's no picnic working by remote control and placing part of your fragile, carefully nurtured, and jealously guarded reputation in someone else's hands. The prospect is about as appealing as hiring a gorilla to dust the displays in a china shop.

2. **Control-centered managers.** All right, let's throw PC-speak to the winds and call 'em control freaks. You probably do anyway. They prefer to be "hands on" all the time, which can drive their employees crazy. ("Bill, don't you think you should tilt your blinds just a little bit more? Your monitor screen shouldn't be in direct sunlight. And when's the last time you backed up your hard drive?")

3. **Skeptics.** Many managers doubt or are apprehensive about employees' abilities or motives, so they're reluctant to give them new or challenging assignments or work that calls for original thinking and independent judgment.

4. **Loners.** These managers, who may be second cousins to perfectionists, have trouble embracing teamwork and putting their faith in others.

5. **Gun-shy.** Some managers have made an honest attempt to delegate meaningful work to a worker sometime in the past, only to see their efforts backfire. The employee may have ruined a job, which caused the manager to get chewed out, which led him or her to take a blood oath not to delegate anything important ever again. The gun-shy manager's motto might be, "Once burned, twice shy."

6. **Uncomfortable with the unexpected.** Managers who prefer predictable, orderly, by-the-book work assignments don't like to delegate, because workers who mishandle assignments may cause some nasty surprises.

7. **Natural autocrats.** Managers who follow the credo "I'm paid to think; you're paid to work" don't delegate anything significant, for a combination of reasons one through six above.

With Teams: Delegate or Die

If you're a team leader, or if your company is moving toward a team-oriented corporate culture, you'll have little choice but to delegate to the members of your team. That's another excellent reason for having this book surgically attached to your body.

Team-based organizations demand that managers relinquish control to an extreme degree and delegate traditional roles and functions such as planning, organizing, directing, and controlling to their teams.

Delegation is thus no longer an option for managers who work in team-based organizations. It's a requirement. You'll be expected to abandon your traditional notions of authority and control to team members to achieve true consensus and install the concept as a part of your corporate culture.

Old-school "I'm paid to think; you're paid to work" managers who refuse to let go *will* be let go, because their Rambo style of management is diametrically opposed to teamwork.

You Can't Hide From Responsibility

Perhaps the most frightening thing about delegating work is that *you're ultimately responsible for what happens.* You can hold the worker accountable for the job or the decision, but *you* handed it down, and you have to face the music if things go awry.

This is one of the most enduring truths in management. If it weren't so, consumers would be suing assembly workers when products went haywire and management would fire them when quality went down the tubes.

In high school, I worked as a stock boy for a retail store—the lowest person on the totem pole. If the place had drawn up an organization chart, I wouldn't even have had honorable mention. Nevertheless, through the dynamics of delegation, I managed to get my boss, the store manager, chastised by the regional manager.

One day, after sweeping the stairway, I forgot to dust off the handrail. The next people down the stairway were the regional manager and store manager—in that order. I was standing at the bottom as the regional manager inspected the palm of his hand, which looked as black as a mine shaft.

"Check this out," he said, displaying his hand to my boss, who began turning several shades of red.

"Damn it," my boss said, turning to me, "you're responsible for wiping down that rail every time you sweep!"

I produced a clean handkerchief and handed it to the regional guy, who shook his head as he looked at my boss. "We can't run this business by blaming stock boys for what happens," he said quietly. "This is *your* store. I hold *you* responsible for everything that goes on under this roof."

So delegation made it possible for the lowest-ranking person in that store to get the highest one reprimanded. (By the way, I never forgot to wipe down that handrail again!)

Your Own Worst Enemy?

The biggest roadblock to effective delegation may be you. You have to attack and conquer your own misgivings and anxiety about the whole thing. Agile managers resolve to do precisely that, however, because they realize that refusing to delegate work retards their growth and careers.

Have you ever seen a sea anchor? Made of canvas and shaped like an airport wind sock, it's thrown overboard to help maintain control in rough seas by creating a drag on the boat.

A sea anchor can be pretty valuable on board a boat, but it has no place in your office. Managers who don't delegate effectively become their own occupational sea anchors, and that can be catastrophic. They create a drag on their own careers, retard their progress, and torpedo their futures.

Agile managers, on the other hand, are accomplished delegators who have taken charge of their professional lives.

Make the Effort

Instinctive delegators, like natural ones, are a fictitious breed. The act of delegating is a solemn transaction between a manager and employee, and it deserves to be treated accordingly. You approach the practice by:

- Selecting carefully which tasks or decisions to keep and which to let go.
- Taking an organized, logical approach to handing off work.
- Communicating the delegated assignment clearly from the worker's point of view.
- Anticipating potential resistance and addressing it effectively.

Each of these actions will be explored in the coming chapters. Let's go!

Chapter One

Delegate to Get Ahead

*"[Well-managed, innovative organizations] give their
people the right to be wrong."*

Laurel Cutler, Vice Chairman, FCB/Leber Katz Partners

"Control freaks don't grow good companies."

Jeffry A. Timmons, Babson College

The Agile Manager was headed for home on Friday night when
he saw a light on in Phil's office. He glanced in. Phil, pasty-faced
as usual, sat amid an extraordinarily messy desk.

"Phil," said the Agile Manager. "It's after 7:00. Aren't you going
home?"

"Nah," said Phil, glancing at the Agile Manager through his
Coke-bottle-bottom lenses. "I've got some stuff to do."

"Do you need more help so we can get you home to your family
quicker?"

"That's the problem. You gave me some help, and it's just created more work."

The Agile Manager put down his briefcase and sat down. "Tell
me about it," he said.

15

Phil sighed. "Well, ever since we hired Judy to help me, it seems I've been busier than ever. I have to check everything she does, of course, and sometimes I have to jump in when something's not going well."

Uh-oh, thought the Agile Manager. The delegator from hell. "Is she more trouble than she's worth?"

"No," said Phil. "Not at all. She's good. But if I don't keep close tabs on her, I don't know what's going on—especially if I could do something a lot faster than she could."

"Uh, Phil," said the Agile Manager slowly. "I want you to do two things. First, go home now. It's the weekend. Second, let's get together Monday morning. I may be able to help you."

Although managers can cite lots of motives for *not* delegating work, there are many more reasons why they should. Let's take a look at the motivations behind delegating work. As you'll see, the arguments that favor delegation outweigh those against it.

Why You Might Not Delegate

It's often easier to find excuses for not doing something than for doing it. When it comes to delegating work, here are some of the all-time favorites.

Lone Ranger Syndrome. (Or, "I'm the only one who can do it right.") Some bosses seem to relish the role of managerial martyr or supervisory Sisyphus (rolling that heavy burden of decisions up the hill every day, only to have it roll back down again). Yet, at the risk of sounding negative, there are hundreds of downsized managers who deluded themselves into believing that they were the only ones who could do their former jobs. If that were true, why were they let go?

Nobody but nobody is indispensable. We might like to fantasize that we are, but take a look around. Somebody's covering for those Lone-Ranger managers who refuse to delegate, which is *prima facie* evidence that they weren't as invaluable as they thought. People retire, die, quit, or are downsized every day, and their jobs get covered somehow. There are no true Lone Rangers in management.

I'm responsible for what happens. You might reprimand, fire, or otherwise make life unpleasant for employees who bungle an assignment, but you still have to answer for their mistakes.

Sure, it's scary. Richard Nixon once said, "I have an absolute rule. I refuse to make a decision that somebody else can make. The first rule of leadership is to save yourself for the big decision. Don't allow your mind to become cluttered with the trivia." When the Watergate slammed shut on his fingers, however, he became a victim of this immutable management truth.

Not to put too fine a point on it, but agile managers have come to terms with this reality. There's some consolation, however: The better you prepare employees for

Repeat this until it sticks: "I'm *not* the only one who can do it, I'm *not* the only one who can do it . . ."

certain tasks and decisions and the more effectively you handle the act of delegation itself, the less worried you'll be about their performance. Is delegation risky? Of course. But this book will help you minimize that risk considerably, which will help you sleep well at night.

I don't have time to teach someone else. Oh, really? If you don't, who will? The higher that pile in your in-basket climbs, and the longer your list of e-mail, the worse your job becomes and the more panicked and overwhelmed you feel. There's virtually never an ideal time to teach an employee how to do a newly delegated task. The best time to begin grooming employees for delegated work is right now. A "better time" will probably never come.

I might delegate myself out of a job. It's natural to worry about making yourself redundant by delegation. If your employees are doing such a great job, who needs you? The answer is your present company—in a higher position, of course.

When an agile manager works for an inept manager, however, the relationship can turn sour. One employee with seventeen years of service used his delegated authority to the maximum, racking up outstanding performance and winning major awards for continuous improvements and cost savings.

Unfortunately, his exceptional achievements simultaneously exposed serious gaps in his boss's performance and opportunities that his boss had either overlooked or failed to exploit.

Strange things started to happen. Inaccurate and forged documents began circulating under his name. Longtime co-workers, fearing guilt by association and damage to their own reputations, stopped talking to him and went out of their way to avoid him. He was cut out of the communications loop. The harassment escalated, and finally he was laid off. The fact that the company ultimately fired his incompetent and malicious boss was little satisfaction.

My people are overloaded already. Well, who isn't? If you can find anybody in your organization who doesn't complain about being too busy, they're probably prime candidates for downsizing.

Although you should be sensitive to your employees' work loads, morale, and protests, you should also realize that most workers feel "too busy" today.

And if you're genuinely overloaded to a point where it's starting to jeopardize your performance (not to mention your health, family relationships, etc.), the fastest way to long-lasting relief (never mind Alka-Seltzer or Maalox) is delegation. You can do it compassionately, sympathetically, and tactfully, but do it!

I hate to lose the credit. If you're in a highly team-oriented organization, it's likely that you're sharing credit for your group's success already. Teamwork isn't compatible with credit thieves and Lone Ranger managers.

Even if your company hasn't adopted teamwork, however, appreciate the wisdom and long-term benefits of sharing credit with your people. The better they look, the better you look. After all, you're responsible, right?

Egotistical credit hogs who let their vanity displace common sense and business judgment can often cost themselves and their companies thousands of dollars.

For example, one ambitious and enthusiastic employee, who worked as second-in-command to the owner of a small consulting firm, built up an exceptional rapport with the company's major client. His boss, overwhelmed by jealousy, decided to assert his presence by raising fees 25 percent. The client, of course, was furious and took the business—which amounted to more than six figures annually—to a competing firm.

Bosses who claim others' ideas as their own, grandstand, and refuse to share the spotlight with their subordinates generate enormous contempt and resentment.

It's a terrible way to manage people. You become an adversary

> ## *B*est *T*ip
>
> Share credit with others. Your people will respect you and work more productively. (And bring you yet more credit.)

instead of a confident leader who earns and deserves your people's respect and loyalty. Since there are more of them than you, your days may be numbered. Given the opportunity, they'll sabotage you and try to bring you down at every turn. Can you blame them?

Why Delegate?

We've looked at reasons why bosses don't delegate. Now how about the other side of the coin: reasons why you should. There are plenty of them, and each one applies to you, no matter where you work or what you do.

Unload routine or noncritical work. As your job expands (as it almost certainly will, because of company growth, downsizing or both), you're called on to do more and more. The less you delegate, the heavier your burden becomes. Eventually your performance is bound to slip, followed perhaps by your health, your personal relationships, and your career—not necessarily in that order.

Best Tip

Delegate to relieve stress and give you time to deal with more strategic issues.

Delegation then becomes a safety valve that can bring you welcome relief from this high-stress, pressure-cooker situation. It liberates you to deal with the non-routine or critical problems that demand concentration and hard mental labor and aren't necessarily governed by policies, procedures, or rules.

This isn't to say, however, that the tasks and decisions you delegate will be considered dull or routine by the people you hand them off to. Decisions that have become standard for you can be challenging and gratifying for your employees, requiring them to cultivate fresh skills and broaden their perspectives in the process.

Get rid of excess managerial baggage. Delegating enables you to step back and see the forest instead of the trees. Managers who allow themselves to be swept away by a tide of trivia often lose perspective and focus. The impact on your long-term growth and career goals can be damaging.

Dedicated delegators know the true value of their time. They're determined to invest it wisely and pursue the best return. This means they focus on decisions, tasks, and issues that are extraordinary or unusual—things that merit their attention and energy. You don't see CEOs hoisting the flag up the flagpole in front of corporate headquarters every morning.

Groom a successor. While incompetent or insecure managers are fretting about delegating themselves out of a job, agile managers are trying to delegate themselves into one—a higher one, that is. Quality organizations (yes, I'm assuming that you work for one) demand depth in management. That means that you won't go anywhere unless you make sure your job can be filled by someone else. That person may be an employee who now works for you.

One of the most time-honored and effective ways to groom a successor is to delegate meaningful work to subordinates. When, through delegation, you require employees to think and act like managers, they *become* managers by the very experience.

Top management, then, may demand that you delegate work as a way to prepare an heir to your throne. Fail to do so, and you may find that you've been moved out instead of up.

In today's business arena, the most upwardly mobile, self-confident managers realize they can't afford not to delegate to their people. Take a look at the managers above your level. It's a safe bet that most of them didn't get where they are by refusing to delegate!

Train your people as part of a career-development program. This overlaps with your need to groom a successor. Delegation makes you a mentor by default. It's a major way to fulfill your moral contract to help your people grow and achieve their own career goals. Training seminars, courses, retreats, etc., all have their value, but delegation is the most enduring and consistently valuable training technique, and it's at your command every working day.

Delegation isn't just a key ingredient in career development; it's also a great way to strengthen job security. When you delegate meaningful tasks and decisions, you help your people increase their versatility. The more versatile they are, the more value they add to your organization—and the harder they are to do without in times of downsizing.

Best Tip

Give meaningful work to your high-potential people. It's the best way to groom an able successor.

Share power with and empower your people. Delegation makes empowerment more than a buzzword. In fact, delegation is the very essence of the concept. Workers on the firing line thrive in a truly empowered organization. That's because their managers have shared the mantle of authority with them by re-laying decisions down to the most appropriate level.

Enhance your credibility as a participative leader. Managers who sow the seeds of authority through delegation reap respect and loyalty from their employees as a result. Participative managers aren't hypocrites. They walk their talk by delegating.

Motivate ambitious employees. Workers who are upwardly mobile welcome opportunities to expand their skills, enhance their résumés, and become qualified for more responsibility.

Delegation, which is actually informal job enlargement, keeps the fire of ambition burning brightly. The bright lights in motivational theory all see delegation as an excellent motivational tool because it:

1. Helps to satisfy ego and esteem needs (Abraham Maslow).
2. Gives employees the opportunity to grow within their present jobs (Frederick Herzberg).
3. Implies trust and confidence, which are hallmarks of a Theory Y manager (Douglas McGregor).

Reduce turnover among your best people. Delegating meaningful work is one way to keep your stars from feeling bored, disillusioned, alienated, and trapped in stale, ordinary, by-the-numbers jobs that they consider beneath their abilities and unworthy of their talent.

Best Tip

Delegate to motivate ambitious employees. That's how you keep good people on the payroll.

Once-enthusiastic employees who don't receive the challenges and growth opportunities they seek (and may have been led to expect when they were recruited) may "vote with their feet" and look for greener pastures. Enjoy the all-around benefits of keeping such valuable human resources on board by keeping their work dynamic and interesting through delegation.

How Well Do You Delegate?

Here's a quick quiz to assess your delegating skills. Answer the following questions yes or no. Don't dwell on them; record your first response.

Yes	No		
		1.	I do many things that my employees should be doing.
		2.	My subordinates seem to have too much time on their hands.
		3.	I should be able to answer any question about what's happening in the department.
		4.	My in-basket and briefcase are usually overflowing.
		5.	My employees tend to solve problems without coming to me.
		6.	My department runs fine when I'm away.
		7.	I get too bogged down with details.
		8.	My employees have enough authority to make most decisions without coming to me.
		9.	I sometimes intrude on my workers' decisions.
		10.	I have prepared someone to take over if I'm away for a week or two.
		11.	I'm buried in paperwork after I've been away for several days.
		12.	I often hand off jobs that I don't like.
		13.	I know what motivates each of my people.
		14.	I'd rather not delegate parts of a task.
		15.	I want my employees to achieve their full potential.
		16.	I worry that people will resent me when I tell them to do things.
		17.	I'm confident that workers won't goof off when my back is turned.
		18.	My employees' performance should be higher than it is.

Yes	No	
		19. I make a special effort to praise people when they do well.
		20. I allow employees to dump work in my lap.
		21. The tasks that I do personally cannot be done by anyone else in my department.
		22. My department has bottlenecks that should be eliminated.
		23. My employees understand what they're supposed to do when I'm not around.
		24. I don't have enough time to plan the work of my department.
		25. I usurp my workers' authority often.
		26. I take too much work home at night.
		27. My job responsibilities intrude on the quality of my ~~family~~ life.
		28. My employees have the training they need to do their jobs well.
		29. I have a list of routine tasks and try to delegate as many as possible.
		30. I encourage my employees to acquire skills and abilities that would prepare them to handle more responsibility.

Scoring: Give one point for each "Yes" for numbers 5, 6, 8, 10, 12, 13, 14, 15, 17, 19, 21, 23, 28, 29, and 30.

Give one point for each "No" for numbers 1, 2, 3, 4, 7, 9, 11, 16, 18, 20, 22, 24, 25, 26, and 27.

Interpretation:

Scores 24–30: You're an agile delegator and a people-oriented leader. Start picking out the furniture for your corner office.

Scores 18–23: You're a so-so delegator who has lots of room for improvement. Analyze the questions you missed and rewrite them as goal statements for your personal growth and development—then start to work on them ASAP!

Scores less than 18: Your inadequate delegation is probably jeopardizing your career and the careers of those who work for you. Buy a second copy of this book to keep beside your bed and read yourself to sleep each night.

The Agile Manager's Checklist

✔ Delegate to:

■ Unload routine or programmed tasks and decisions;
■ Free yourself from administrative trivia;
■ Groom a successor;
■ Help subordinates develop their careers;
■ Share power and empower people;
■ Enhance your reputation as a participative leader;
■ Motivate ambitious employees;
■ Reduce turnover among your best performers.

✔ Identify and analyze your delegation-related attitudes, habits, and skills. Use tools such as the self-assessment test at the end of this chapter to identify specific areas that need improvement.

Chapter Two

Delegate the Right Jobs

"First and foremost as a manager or supervisor . . . your job is to get things done through other people. . . . You are paid to manage, not perform every task."

MARY ANN ALLISON, VICE PRESIDENT, CITICORP, AND ERIC ALLISON, FINANCIAL WRITER

"Give up control, even if it means the employees have to make some mistakes."

FRANK FLORES, CEO, MARSDEN REPRODUCTIONS

". . . So then we had to call them all back to get new numbers. At that point, I told her to forget it—that I'd do it myself."

The Agile Manager pursed his lips, then began to speak. "Phil, first thing is this: You have to trust someone to do a job. If for some reason it goes wrong, have them do it again. When you yank a job, two things happen: You've just added an item to your own to-do list. Second, you've sent a message: 'You weren't up to this task.' You may even send this message: 'You're stupid.' I don't have to tell you that either one isn't motivating."

HOW TO

He continued. "Remember a few years ago when I had you do a presentation to the Rembrandt Graphics Group? You came back and—"

"I remember," interrupted Phil. "You were perturbed, to put it lightly, that I hadn't covered a couple of important points."

"Right," said the Agile Manager. "And, I'll tell you, it was all I could do to keep from calling Annie over there to fill her in on the rest. I was afraid we'd lose the contract. But I sat on my hands and asked you to follow up on all matters until we got the contract. And you know what? We did. And you got some extra confidence in yourself and our work. And I became more confident that I could let you loose on important tasks. Which, not coincidentally, freed me up for other things."

Phil seemed to be looking at a distant cloud through the window. He came back to Earth abruptly. "Can we talk again tomorrow? I have an idea."

"Any time," said the Agile Manager.

If you've read this far, you must be sold on the value of delegating work. Congratulations. Now it's time to think about which jobs or decisions you should hold on to and which might be best to hand off. Your choices will be influenced by at least three factors: your boss, your subordinates, and the length of time you've been in your present job and/or company.

Gauge Your Boss's Attitude

The perceptions, prejudices, and circumstances of the person you work for can have a significant impact on both what and how you delegate. More specifically, think about your manager's attitude and feelings toward:

Accountability. There's a domino principle at work here. The length of the leash that your boss is on will likely affect how much slack he or she is willing to give you. That, in turn, may affect which tasks and decisions you're comfortable handing off to your people and which ones you may feel compelled to keep for yourself.

Communications. If your boss insists on frequent contact and fast answers when problems arise, weigh those inclinations accordingly when delegating. Make sure you can reach the necessary people quickly in case a real or imagined crisis comes up.

People. Is your boss a Theory X manager who usually expects the worst from people or a Theory Y manager who tends to expect the best? Managers who work for a Theory X boss often keep their delegating activities under the table to avoid objections or criticism from higher up. Those who have Theory Y bosses can be more overt, however, because their managers usually advocate delegation and place more confidence in others.

✳ **Delegation as a management tool.** If you work for a confirmed delegator who's relatively comfortable handing down authority, he or she may be more at ease with your delegating, because the two of you are cast from the same mold. By contrast, a control-freak boss may be skeptical about if not firmly opposed to your actions, which means you may have to downplay your enthusiasm for delegation and keep your activities under wraps.

| Best Tip

Delegate things that will improve the skills of your people and prepare them for higher-level work.

Assess your boss's position on all these factors before you decide how extensively to delegate to your people, how you'll communicate delegated assignments to them, what channels of communication you'll establish for feedback and follow-up, and how widely you should publicize what you've done within your organization. It's not politically savvy to appear philosophically at odds with your boss—even if, in fact, you are.

Gauge Your Subordinates' Skills and Abilities

There'll be more on this later. For now, let's just say that you need to evaluate each of your employees objectively so you can decide:

- Which of your present tasks and decisions some workers are capable of handling with little or no preparation or supervision.
- Which activities certain employees are likely to do successfully with a moderate degree of direction, coaching, and support from you.
- What type of work is most compatible with each individual's likes and dislikes. (Although it's not always possible to accommodate workers this way, it helps to understand what kinds of work each one enjoys and which tasks or decisions each would prefer to avoid in cases where you're able to give them a choice.)
- What management functions your workers need added experience with to increase their expertise, prepare themselves for more meaningful work, and shore up areas that you and they have targeted for improvement.

Evaluate Your Tenure

Don't jump the gun. If you're new to your job, department, or company, take your time before delegating anything. You need to get your arms around the situation and clearly understand the repercussions or impact of work you might hand down.

The longer you've been in your position, however, the better you know the lay of the land. You know the values and principles that drive your corporate culture, your boss's idiosyncrasies and attitude toward delegation, and what makes your people tick.

This corporate intelligence enables you to decide which work you can delegate, which work you should delegate, which employees are best suited for it, and what response you can expect from your own boss and members of higher management.

Delegating Decisions Versus Delegating Tasks

You may have noticed that I've referred to decisions and tasks separately, and for good reason. They're both "work," but they're not synonymous.

When you delegate decisions, you give people the ongoing right to act in your place or on your behalf. They become your agent or attorney.

When you delegate tasks, you hand down physical jobs (or parts of them) that may not demand much decision-making talent or finesse. These include such things as gathering information or materials for an upcoming speech, preparing a monthly productivity report, reorganizing a data base, or installing new software on your department's computers.

> **Best Tip**
>
> Delegating decisions saves you more time, in the long run, than delegating tasks.

Delegating decisions often creates more time for you than delegating tasks. That's because making decisions typically involves time-consuming steps such as analyzing a problem, developing potential solutions, gathering information about each alternative, and the like—all of which take time and mental labor.

What to Delegate

Don't delegate only junk or trivia and save all the fun for yourself. That offends employees' sense of fair play and equity. They'll resist you and resent you, which should hardly be a surprise. Nobody likes to be dumped on.

Delegate the good stuff as well—pleasant tasks, win-win decisions, and work that you yourself might enjoy doing. That confirms to workers your interest in helping them grow and be productive. They'll respect you for it, and you'll find you've enhanced the spirit of camaraderie and teamwork within your group.

Delegate tasks and decisions that are relatively "programmed" to less experienced people who may not be ready to work under laissez-faire conditions. This might be work that doesn't demand a great deal of discretion or creative thinking because it falls within established organizational guidelines and is governed by policies, procedures, and rules. That's not to say, however, that such work won't be satisfying to the employees you're giving it to. They'll probably welcome the change of pace and escape from their normal routine.

In addition, delegate fairly. Try to balance the level of difficulty and discretion in the work you hand down among your employees so you won't be accused of playing favorites.

Failing to do this creates friction and resentment among your people, some of whom will believe that others are getting a better deal. Those who think they usually get the short end of the stick will resent their more favored co-workers—and you.

Get Specific

Building a "hit list" of tasks and decisions that you intend to delegate, and evaluating potential candidates for that work, gives you a tangible sense of progress. The simple physical act of setting these things down on paper reveals light at the end of the tunnel and helps you see that the administrative mountain you've sworn to conquer may not be so intimidating after all.

Start by assessing yourself and your work circumstances by asking these questions:

1. Might some of your employees be better qualified than you to handle certain tasks and decisions that you've kept on your agenda? If so, write down their names and match them with the appropriate work.

2. Which employees have pointedly asked you for opportunities to expand their skills, learn more, and generally increase their value to your department and company? This is an index of their ambition and willingness to be delegated to.

3. What routine clerical or administrative activities consume most of your time yet produce the least benefits? These nickel-and-dime operations should definitely be given to someone else.

You can usually pinpoint chores that most deserve to be delegated by analyzing daily or weekly activity logs, to-do lists, desk calendar jottings, meeting agendas, and your schedule for the past several weeks. Identify standard items that pop up routinely (trips to the restroom and coffee breaks don't count) and:

1. List them on a piece of paper.
2. Estimate the amount of time each item requires.
3. Rank them in order from the most time-consuming to the least time-consuming.
4. Construct a priority list of the things you need to delegate most, focusing on the items that consume most of your time. (They're the things you need to get rid of.)
5. Match your priority list with your subordinates' skills and abilities, considering the factors mentioned on page 29.
6. Celebrate! Why? Because you've just produced a delegation action plan.

Now you can stop feeling like you've been trying juggle a handful of feathers. You've identified specific tasks and decisions that are chewing up most of your time, aligned them with your most likely delegates, and are about to take the next major step: dealing with the mechanics of the process.

And that just happens to be the subject of the next chapter.

The Agile Manager's Checklist

✔ Gauge your boss's attitude toward accountability and delegation. It may affect your choice of what to delegate.
✔ Evaluate the work you want to hand down in light of your subordinates' skills and abilities.
✔ Know your job and organization. It'll be easier to know which work to keep and which to delegate.
✔ Understand that you'll probably save more time delegating decisions than delegating tasks.

Chapter Three

The Basics of
Successful Delegation

"I'm not allowed to drive the train; the whistle I can't blow.
I'm not allowed to say how far this string of cars can go.
I cannot holler, 'All aboard!' or even ring the bell.
But let the damn thing jump the track, and see who catches hell."

ANON.

" . . . And so I plan to let her do the whole job. I won't take it back." Phil leaned back in his chair, quite pleased with himself.

The Agile Manager searched for something nice to say. *"That's the right attitude, Phil."* He glanced down again at the sheaf of papers Phil had handed him. The title page read, *"Specifications and Purposes for Delegated Research Projects #101 and 102."*

"But I wonder if this is the right approach." He turned to the three-page checklist at the end of the report. *"You see, Phil, you've essentially done the job already by sequencing the activities, telling her where to look for data, how to write the report, and everything else."*

"Right," said Phil. *"That way, I know things will turn out right."*

"How long did you spend on this?"

"Oh, not long—maybe four or five hours."

The Agile Manager bit his lip and looked at the ceiling briefly. "Phil," he said finally. "Part of delegating is letting the person figure out how to do the work. There's a great advantage when you do that. You—the delegator—might learn something. It could be new information you hadn't thought of, or even a new approach."

"But I know what I want—that's why I wrote it all up." *Phil tilted his head at a forty-five-degree angle, as if it might help him better understand the Agile Manager's reasoning.*

"All I can say is that I learn new things from all of you when I ask you to do things and turn you loose without too many boundaries. But the other thing, Phil, is that you spent five hours on this. I'm guessing the two jobs together might take someone seven or eight. And your time is a lot more expensive than Judy's."

I wish they had taught me some of this stuff in engineering school, thought Phil.

You've spent some time thinking about what you're going to delegate and to whom. Now it's probably hard to keep from charging out of your office faster than a squirrel on amphetamines, delegating with wild abandon.

Best to cool it for a bit and think through the mechanics of the process so you don't go riding off in all directions.

Talk to Yourself

You need to explain to yourself your rationale and motives for the jobs or decisions you're handing down before you can explain them clearly to anyone else. Do that by asking yourself, "Self, why are you delegating this?" The answer should be fairly easy, because of the list you made in the last chapter. It's good practice to analyze your motives by asking yourself a direct question, however, to make sure you have your reasons clear and your delegation ducks in a row.

Once you've examined your logic for leaks and plugged any holes with this test run, you can move ahead and set up meetings with your employees with some assurance that they'll go smoothly. But before you do, let's look at a few other considerations.

Delegate to the Proper Level

Workers who rub shoulders with problems and issues every day are the most logical people to resolve them. (How's that for a flash of insight?)

Armchair "experts" who stand on their swivel chairs and view the situation through binoculars are usually in the worst position to deal with it. It's like playing chess blindfolded. You may think you know what's going on, but you can't be sure.

Jan Carlzon, former CEO of airline company SAS (Sweden), is a staunch advocate of this principle. He said, "[In our company] problems are solved on the spot, as soon as they arise. No front line employee has to wait for a supervisor's permission."

Best Tip
Before you delegate, explain to yourself exactly why you're handing off a task or decision.

If there's a common bond among companies with legendary reputations for customer service and satisfaction, it's higher managers who insist that problems be solved at the lowest possible level and give people at that level the authority to do so. You can do the same—and reap the same benefits.

Choose the Best Person for the Task

Delegation, as you know by now, calls for more than just picking some warm body that's currently available. By following an orderly, thoughtful selection routine you can choose subordinates whose skills are most compatible with the job or pick those who stand to benefit most from the experience.

Compare the task with the candidates. We touched on this in chapter two. Now it's time for some details.

Many supervisors underestimate the importance of this step and/or overlook key aspects of the job and potential candidates they might delegate to. Consider the following factors:

1. *How close is the deadline?* Rush jobs call for time-oriented workers who can be counted on to come through under pressure. Consider available employees in light of their ability to manage themselves and their sense of responsibility both to themselves and to you. The tighter the deadline, the more you'll need to choose a conscientious worker who will do the right thing—and do it on time.

2. *How much coordination is needed?* Delegate to consensus-builders assignments that demand lots of coordination or cooperation among colleagues or departments. Jobs that call for little interaction with other departments, however, might be delegated safely to your more headstrong, less-diplomatic subordinates.

3. *How will the job help the person grow?* Here's an excellent chance to help satisfy employees' training-and-development needs. Identify subordinates who would benefit most from this particular assignment. Consider, for example, the degree of challenge involved in the task; how much initiative, judgment, or discretion it calls for; and how well it will help the candidate develop written or spoken communication skills.

4. *How much innovation is involved?* Highly innovative assignments call for dreamers more than doers—people who, like the bird who built a nest with a hole in the bottom, thrive on creativity but detest responsibility. On the other hand, tasks that involve a standard routine or plain old "grunt work" are best given to detail-minded systems builders who enjoy doing work that's been laid out for them.

In addition to the above, take time to weigh such factors as enthusiasm, drive, and desire. Employees who get excited about learning skills and mastering new techniques may do a better job than their more apathetic co-workers.

Likewise, consider each candidate's determination to grow, meet challenges, and acquire new experience.

Finally, ask yourself which person(s) really seem to want the assignment and perhaps have told you so. Other things being equal, enthusiasm, ambition, and desire deserve to be acknowledged and rewarded.

What if several people are qualified for a job? This is a welcome dilemma, but one that must be handled fairly in order to preserve high morale. One solution is to let the employees themselves decide who will get the job. This tactic, while admittedly frustrating, gives them experience with consensus building, compromise, and group dynamics. Make sure to clarify, however, that you've left the decision up to them for those reasons, and not because you're reluctant to make it yourself or exercise leadership.

Best Tip

Pick eager-to-learn employees to do key jobs. They'll do them better and with a lot more enthusiasm.

An obvious alternative is to pick the person yourself. If you do, make sure to promise those who were passed over that they'll get the next assignments that come up.

You might also let several equally qualified subordinates tackle the project as a team instead of assigning it to one alone.

What if there's no clear choice? If there's no clear standout after you've analyzed the task and candidates, consider giving the job to the person (or perhaps a team of co-workers) who seems to need the experience most and/or possesses most of the skills that the job demands. Relative motivation may be a deciding factor here, too.

Once you've made your decision, explain its rationale to the runners-up. This action is important, because it minimizes claims of favoritism or discrimination. Be sure that everyone understands the criteria you used to make your selection and the reasons why you chose whom you did.

Keep Jobs Intact When Possible

Delegating a complete task or decision lock, stock, and barrel simplifies your life. You won't have any remnants of it hanging from your office ceiling like a colony of bats, intimidating you and diverting your attention from more important things.

This policy also benefits employees you've delegated to, because they can do the entire job from start to finish instead of having to monitor and coordinate various details that have been retained by you or farmed out to several other people. Moreover, workers receive satisfaction from finishing a job and achieving closure. It's intensely gratifying to be able to wrap up an assignment in every aspect and check it off your agenda.

Best Tip

Keep jobs whole when you delegate them. You'll worry less, and employees will enjoy the job more.

Several years ago, I interviewed the owner of a local engine-rebuilding company for a consumer article and enjoyed hearing his opinion about keeping jobs intact within his shop.

"The same employees who pull the engines out of the cars install them after they've been rebuilt," he said, "so they start and finish the process. They like that. After the block and heads have been machined and reconditioned, the engine is put together with new internal parts by one of several assemblers. I could break that work down into an assembly-line system, but we're not a high-volume company, and I'd rather have one person do the whole job. That way I know who to hold accountable if there's a problem, and my engine builders have the satisfaction of assembling the entire engine themselves instead of doing some menial task."

Focus On Results, Not Methods

Plan to tell your delegates the results you want. Don't tell them how to achieve the results.

This is one of the most critical aspects of the delegation process and one that's most difficult for managers to accept. It can't be emphasized strongly enough. In fact, it's a good idea to have it tattooed backward on your forehead so you'll see it every time you look in a mirror.

Concern yourself with ends, not means; what you expect, not how to achieve it; outcomes, not inputs.

Think about it: As long as your employees stay within basic organizational boundaries such as budget, policies, and procedures, and as long as they follow your general guidelines, should you really care how they approach the job? If you do, you have another self-imposed barrier to overcome.

Effective delegators are *macro*managers. They don't clutter up their minds and harass their employees with superfluous nit-picking. They don't fret over the details of the assignment or sweat the small stuff. They don't set out to create clones of themselves.

Micromanagers do all of those things, which means they haven't really delegated at all. They're still preoccupied with how the employee is going to handle the decision or task they think they've delegated. The anxiety and concern hang over their heads, derailing their trains of thought and interrupting their concentration. These folks are baby sitters in business suits. They create false hope in their employees and insult and disappoint them with the illusion of authority.

Best Tip

Tell your delegates what result you want. Don't tell them how to do the job. Their ingenuity will surprise you.

Create boundaries, not barriers. Make sure to outline the limits of the employee's authority and carefully define what he or she may not do, but don't prescribe how to reach the goals you've agreed on. Leave the approach and techniques to the employee's discretion. Managers who do this are often astonished at their employees' creativity and ingenuity.

There are many routes to the same destination. Do your employees the favor of letting them find their own, without forcing them to take you along as a navigator.

Top management at one company that had to pare its budget by a sizable amount delegated the decision to its bottom-level employees instead of sharpening the layoff ax. The goal was simple: to save money. "If you can save what we need to save and still keep your jobs, fine," management said. "We'll listen to anything."

Employees voluntarily cut their hours so that everyone would have a job, and cost-cutting suggestions came out of the woodwork. Because management focused on the end (saving money) instead of the means (how to do it), employees were happy to help reach that goal in ways that kept everyone employed.

Explain the Assignment's Value

If you're planning to delegate a really, *really* trivial task, one that's so patently basic that it wouldn't tax the administrative powers of an amoeba, don't try to inflate its importance by describing it in glowing terms. It'll only sound dumb, and your worker will think you're a jerk.

When an assignment is important, say so. But don't inflate the value of a trivial task. The person will resent it (and you).

One of my first bosses in industry announced grandly a "big assignment" he had planned for me and how we'd meet to discuss it the next day. Wow! I could hardly wait for morning. This impressive assignment turned out to be an absurd clerical chore so far beneath my qualifications that it was an insult. I was both disappointed and furious that he had raised my hopes with all the false hype.

When an assignment carries some real weight, however, make sure to point out its value and meaning to your organization, your department, and the employee. Don't assume that workers will understand or appreciate its long-term impact automatically.

There can be many hidden benefits, such as:

- Expanding the employee's skills,
- Filling an important void in your team's capabilities,
- Addressing one or more areas that were targeted for improvement in a career-development plan,
- Grooming the person for a possible promotion or a new position that's about to be created,
- Helping the worker acquire experience that provides some welcome insulation against future layoffs.

In addition, tasks that you may consider commonplace may seem far from trivial to the worker you're about to delegate to. Perhaps they're ordinary only because you've done them so often for so long. What's "routine" is relative.

For example, I relish discussing delegation principles and techniques, motivational theories, decision making, and successful freelance writing practices with groups of thirty to one hundred people. It's exhilarating, it's fun, and it's somewhat routine because I've done it for a number of years.

To delegate such an assignment to an inexperienced associate, however, might trigger a coronary. So be sure to look at things from your employee's point of view.

Tell It Like It Is

In the same vein, avoid dressing up extremely difficult tasks as "challenges" and laying them on a hapless worker. And use the word "challenge" sparingly, please. So many Pollyanna managers use it as a euphemism for "problem" that people's suspicions are aroused as soon as they hear it. When you say "challenge," they may hear:

- "A problem the size of Texas,"
- "Major-league trouble,"
- "Bad news,"
- "You're about to be dumped on again,"
- "Get ready to put in some eighty-hour weeks,"

- "Postpone your vacation," or
- "Refill your Valium prescription."

One of my bosses in industry, whom I privately called "Challenging Charlie," worked that way. Charlie never delegated a problem. He delegated a "challenge," pronouncing the word in resonant and reverent tones, like George S. Patton addressing his troops. Those of us who worked for him used to grimace, pull on our hip boots or roll up our trousers when we heard another "challenge" coming.

Garbage is garbage and problems are problems, sugarcoated or not. If you call them what they are, at least your people will respect you for it.

It's doubly insulting to be asked to do the impossible by a boss who belongs to the genus *clueless ignoramus*. One computer wizard was delegated the task of installing a network, complete with hardware and software, in his relatively computer-illiterate department.

The next day, his computer-illiterate boss delegated another "little task": summarizing everything the department's employees needed to know about the network and its software on a single sheet of paper. The worker was absolutely thunderstruck. His boss was adamant. Moreover, she insisted that he could only allocate one hour per employee for training. He quit three weeks later.

Delegate Appropriate Authority

If possible, plan to give the person enough authority to do the job without having to "get your approval," "touch base," "check with you first," or otherwise interrupt whatever it is you're doing.

Fail to do this, and you frustrate yourself, your employee, and any other people the employee has to work with on the assignment.

Moreover, your worker looks like a flunky or the good half of a good guy/bad guy tag team. Have you ever tried to buy a car from a salesperson who always had to "check with the boss" on your offer and every counteroffer you made throughout the deal?

While this may be part of the head games that are sometimes played in car sales, it makes the person you're dealing with look useless and awkward, and it's intensely aggravating. I wonder how many deals have been lost because irritated customers refused to tolerate such back-and-forth nonsense.

Once I was wrapping up a weekend-long strategy meeting for a major consulting project I had undertaken. I thought everything had been resolved and agreed upon. Then the manager I had dealt with exclusively said, "Of course, you understand I'll have to run all this by the president of the company on Monday for his OK. I'll get back to you."

Best Tip

Make sure employees have the resources—time, money, assistance— they need to do a job properly.

At that moment, I realized he was playing the good-guy role, like the warm and fuzzy, highly sensitive interrogator in a television cop series. ("Just you and me, baby! I'm looking out for you. Try to work with me here!")

Lesson learned? I never relied on his word or authority from that point on. Before future meetings, I confirmed that I was dealing with the executive who had genuine clout by asking, "Do you have the power to bind the agreement we're trying to reach? If you don't, there's no point in my coming—even if you're paying the bill."

Round Up the Resources

Part of any delegating job involves rounding up the right resources. This means gathering whatever the employee needs to succeed with the assignment: equipment, assistants, budget money, floor space, time, and anything else.

Don't expect the worker to build a Lexus using a screwdriver, pliers, and parts from a '58 Rambler. Success in any venture depends on adequate resources; you can't win the Kentucky Derby with a jackass.

Expect Mistakes

Finally, understand that mistakes are bound to happen. They're part of the process anytime a person tries to master something new, and they're an invaluable and positive part of learning.

Positive, you ask? Absolutely. Mistakes help willing delegates discover what approaches don't work, or don't work well, and thus should be ruled out or modified. Said one occasional philosopher (whose name graces the cover of this book), "People can't buy wisdom all at once. They have to pay as they go, and the price they pay is called experience."

Thomas Edison conducted some 50,000 fruitless experiments in his quest to invent a new storage battery. When someone remarked about this dismaying chain of failures that appeared to produce no results, Edison said, "Results? Why, I have gotten a lot of results! I know 50,000 things that won't work."

Do you remember at least one former manager or mentor who allowed you to "fail forward" by making honest mistakes? You probably owe that person a debt of gratitude, and now it's payback time. Honest mistakes are the product of honest efforts. When you tolerate them, you help your employees advance by their own initiative and grow from within.

The Agile Manager's Checklist

✔ Delegate to the right level, and try to keep jobs intact.
✔ Tell people the results you expect, then let them obtain them any way they want to.
✔ Allow your workers to "fail forward." Accept honest mistakes as part of the learning process.
✔ Make sure your employees know what career benefits they can expect from the job you've delegated.
✔ Give employees the resources and authority it takes to do jobs right.

Chapter Four

Communicate the Assignment

"I know you believe you understand what you think I said. However, I'm not sure you realize that what you heard is not what I meant."

ANONYMOUS

"The meaning of words is not in the words, it is in us."

S. I. HAYAKAWA

"That's the result I'm looking for," said Phil.

Judy looked at him quizzically, waiting for the rest. When she realized he was finished, she said, "How should I go about it?"

"That's for you to figure out," said Phil. "I know I've always directed your work before, but I think you're ready to make some of your own decisions." He said the words slowly, as if they were made of glue.

Judy thought, This is great! But a thought darkened her elation. "What if I get stuck?"

"I'm here for you. It's not like I'm setting you adrift in a row boat. You can come talk to me about it anytime you want."

"Sounds great," she said with a big smile, getting up to leave.

"Hang on," said Phil. "Is there anything I haven't been clear about?"

Judy sank back into the chair. "Uh . . . you thought I should limit my research to the electronics and telecommunications industries, right?"

"Those are the most likely places to look, but you might also check out . . ."

You've explored the motivations for delegating, looked at several criteria for deciding what work to keep and what to let go, and examined the major mechanics of the delegation process.

Now it's time to hold a meeting with the employee to explain the job to be done. This meeting is the foundation for success—but only if you keep the elements of this chapter in mind.

Call a Meeting

Schedule a private, uninterrupted conference to discuss each assignment with each person. Private meetings have several benefits:

- A formal meeting gives your conversation and your decision to delegate the seriousness they deserve. A solemn attitude should rub off on your employee. Seeming flippant or cavalier about the work you're assigning implies that it's not that important. Be serious if you want to be taken seriously.

- Meeting with people individually personalizes your decision and helps you assess their concern, degree of commitment, and other factors that may affect how well they carry out assignments.

- Individual, private meetings minimize gossip and speculation over the grapevine about what you've decided to delegate, why you're doing so, and why you chose the people you did. Holding a group meeting to discuss your decisions and distribute assignments could provoke irrelevant discussion and isolated debates and objections about your reasons for matching up the work and workers as you did.

It's usually better to talk about these things with your employees one-on-one and take care of miscellaneous whining, griping, questions, or challenges later on an individual basis. This is especially true if your action is likely to provoke controversy and perhaps a general uprising if announced to a group. It's the divide-and-conquer principle of management.

Provide Clear Directions

The most important thing in delegating is to be clear from the start.

Do you give clear directions? Of course you do! All managers do! Just ask any of them. You betcha, they'll say. But if you ask some of the people working for them, you might get a very different answer—and one that's not exactly G-rated, if you know what I mean.

Schedule a private meeting to delegate a job. It helps communicate the importance of the matter.

"Clear" means *clear from the employee's point of view.* That means you have to know each of your employees as individuals, and that takes some hard mental labor. Here's just a sample of the questions you need to ask if you want to get your point across clearly:

1. *Is there a potential language barrier?* If your native language is English, for example, and your employee's native language is Spanish or Flemish, it's possible that each of you won't grasp the other's nuances, references, inflections, or idioms. If you suspect difficulties with language, avoid using slang, buzz words, and even gestures that may be misinterpreted or not understood at all.

One manager wrapped up a delegation conference with a new hire from South America by giving him the "OK" sign (or so he thought)—a circled thumb and index finger. The worker went ballistic! In his culture, that gesture means "go screw yourself."

2. *What can I do to make this employee feel comfortable asking me*

questions? Jamie may feel at ease, but Paul may not. It's part of your job to know which workers fit into which category. Although agile managers want everyone to feel comfortable about asking them questions, there'll always be a few reluctant workers who need reassurance and encouragement to speak their minds when they don't understand. Don't assume that your instructions are "self-explanatory."

3. *Do we share the same educational level?* You walk a fine line here. While it's insulting to talk down to people, it's bewildering to them when you talk over their heads.

There's no slick formula to help you choose words and examples that your employee understands. What's scary sometimes is that some people will say they understand when in fact they don't have a clue. (One military officer, testifying in defense of a court-martialed colleague, was asked if the colleague ever displayed any signs of moral turpitude. The officer replied, "He's the finest example of moral turpitude I've ever met.")

Best Tip
Use plain, simple language when explaining an assignment. Draw a picture or model if need be.

Use plain language, or, as one good ol' boy buddy of mine says, "Don't let your education get in the way of what you're trying to say."

4. *Should I give this particular employee a model or some other tangible aid that demonstrates the kind of results I expect?* Some people learn better by seeing than by listening. It's called "cognitive style." If you're talking to someone who seems to be highly visual, make sure to show as well as tell.

5. *Do I have any speech patterns or idiosyncrasies that might be roadblocks to understanding?* While these can be tough to analyze without some outside advice, they can undermine your effectiveness. For example, are you compelled to fill up pauses between sentences with distracting sounds ("ah," "um", "er,") or

worked-to-death crutch words and phrases such as "hey," "you know," "right?," "man," and—perhaps the most detested, over-used, and ridiculous of all—"like"?

One of the most frustrating managers I ever worked with was a fellow we all called "Mumbles." Whenever we sat down to discuss an assignment, he spoke in a tortured series of grunts, incomplete sentences, and various other disjointed utterances that left everyone totally bewildered. His speech was the oral equivalent of a fill-in-the-blanks test. If that weren't bad enough, he never looked you in the eye. He studied the toes of his shoes, instead, while he talked.

The overall impression you got was that of a dementia patient who had wandered into the building from a nearby nursing home. To give the devil his due, this guy was good at what he did. He was never able to delegate successfully, however, because the rest of us had a terrible time under-standing what he was talking about. If we asked him to repeat what he said, he merely turned up the volume and mumbled louder.

6. *What haven't I been clear about that we should discuss some more?* That's not a question to ask your-self. It's one to ask your employee

> **Best Tip**
>
> Ask again and again if neces-sary: "What haven't I been clear about? What don't you understand about the job?"

as a capstone before you wrap up your delegation meeting. It's a terrific idea, because when you ask this, you admit frankly that you probably weren't as clear as you could have been. That makes it easier for your employee to ask for more details without wor-rying about offending you or seeming to be dumb.

Define the Limits

This is a biggie. Your people must know how far they can go without your approval.

Weigh the merits of describing their discretion and authority in writing. Doing so isn't meant to insult the worker's intelligence. It's simply sound communication practice to send a vital message by both means: speaking and writing. For instance, you may want to spell out for workers:

1. The dollar amounts they're authorized to approve or spend without involving you.
2. Examples of issues or problems they may act on immediately, those they should inform you about after the fact, and those that they should discuss with you before proceeding (more on this in the next section).
3. Specific "delegatable" tasks and duties from your job description that you're transferring to them. Provide a list.
4. Circumstances in which they may use your name and act in your place instantly. ("Darlene Owens, the general manager, has authorized me to extinguish any diners whose clothing catches fire from the Cherries Jubilee without obtaining her approval.")

Give Them a Role to Live Up To

When you discuss the assignment with the employee, highlight aspects of the project that may be somewhat troublesome. Express your faith in the employee's ability to cope, however, with these potential difficulties and benefit from the experience. Each of us grows by being asked to stretch beyond our present limits. You compliment your people when you expect more from them than they think they're capable of.

Last but not least, don't give the impression that the job's a sink-or-swim proposition. Be prepared to coach and be more accessible to marginally qualified workers, while taking care not to let them shift decisions onto your shoulders or use your availability as a crutch.

Set a Level of Authority

Have you ever heard yourself or someone you know complain, "My boss holds me accountable for results, but he didn't give me enough authority," or "I did exactly what she told me to, then she said I did it wrong"?

The Results Group, a Santa Rosa, California, consulting firm that specializes in organizational effectiveness training, helps managers keep their workers out of that bind by describing six categories of authority. These can help you establish the degree of authority you truly mean to delegate:

1. Look into the issue and give me all the facts. I'll decide.
2. Look into the issue and let me know the pros and cons. Recommend an action for my approval.
3. Look into the issue and let me know the pros and cons. We'll decide what to do together.
4. Look into the issue and tell me what you intend to do before you proceed.
5. Take appropriate action and tell me what happened.
6. Take appropriate action; no need to contact me further.

Figure 4-1 on the next page shows the Assignment/Delegation Form this company recommends to its clients.

Here's what can happen when you don't set a specific level of authority for a job.

A worker in one large company described the report-writing assignments he was delegated this way: Once he's written a report, he's required to give it to his boss to edit. When they finally agree on its wording and content (which may require several revisions), the report then goes to his boss's boss for editing. The report then goes back down again, where each change the higher boss made is reviewed by the two of them.

Best Tip

Show that you believe in the delegate's ability to do the job. Your faith provides a force that helps the person succeed.

They may recommend changes to his changes, of course, so the report may be shuttled back and forth several times. As if that weren't enough, a third boss was also involved—one who

ASSIGNMENT/DELEGATION FORM

Date: ___/___/___

Delgated to: _____   From: _____

ASSIGNMENT:

IMPORTANT CONSIDERATIONS: (Facts, do's/dont's, limits, parameters, who to involve)

LEVEL OF AUTHORITY YOU HAVE:

- Look into this issue; give me all the facts so I can make a decision.
- Look into this issue; let me know the alternatives (pros and cons); recommend one for my approval.
- Look into this issue; let me know the alternatives (pros and cons); then you and I will decide together.
- Look into this issue; let me know what you intend to do before you proceed.
- Take appropriate action; let me know what the outcome was.
- Take appropriate action; no further contact with me is needed.

THE FINAL PRODUCT I EXPECT IS:

TIMELINE:

Assignment given on: _____/_____/_____

Meet with me for a progress report on: _____/_____/_____

Other intermediate steps:

The final product is due on: _____/_____/_____

Figure 4-1: The Results Group's Delegation Form
(Used with permission.)

was really eager to demonstrate that he was on top of things. The manager has to run the report by him as well. Any changes this boss makes naturally require approval by the other two bosses.

Unfortunately, overall effectiveness suffers. By failing to set a specific level and degree of authority, higher managers have allowed the job of writing these reports to eat up a great deal of the lower managers' time. Meanwhile, the person who's likely to be the best candidate for the job—the employee who wrote the original draft—ends up sitting on the sidelines.

Establish a Deadline

Giving somebody a job with a deadline of "yesterday" isn't fair and can be unnerving. Remember, this is the first the employee has heard about these marvelous delegation plans you've been drawing up during the past several days.

If you're delegating work that's fairly routine, covered by procedures, and well within the scope of the employee's ability, your worker may not need much prep time—perhaps just a day or two. If the assignment is extremely detailed or complex or requires extensive preparation and orientation, give the worker some attitude-adjustment time. It's likely that her calendar is filled already. As they say in Washington every four years or so, provide for an "orderly transition."

Agree on an end date if the job has a definite time frame. This will help your worker plan, coordinate, and prioritize this task in light of his or her present workload. Forewarn the employee about possible changes to the schedule as well.

Get a Commitment

Get your employee's pledge to do a sound and conscientious job with whatever tasks or decisions you're handing down. Make certain that workers understand your respective roles: You're ultimately responsible for what happens, but you hold all of them fully accountable for the results and consequences of their performance and decisions.

Obtain one additional commitment from your delegates as well: A commitment to always, *always,* ALWAYS ask questions if they're confused or unclear about something.

You've probably read the motto somewhere in your company, "Stupid questions are easier to handle than dumb mistakes." No agile manager would dream of labeling a worker's question "stupid," of course. The point is that your employees must feel free to speak with you any time if they believe they need more guidance or information.

Follow-up and Reporting

The category of delegation you've chosen will dictate what follow-up methods you'll use. With Level Six delegation ("Take appropriate action; no need to contact me further") you won't use any at all.

Short of that, however, tell your employee what follow-up methods you plan to use and the formats and frequency of any reports that may be necessary. You have plenty of options here, ranging in formality from official meetings and oral or written reports to daily or weekly activity logs, periodic question-and-answer sessions, teleconferencing, e-mail, voice mail, and informal discussions in the hallway or during lunch. Keep paperwork and face-to-face meeting time at a minimum; go for electronic communications whenever possible.

Best Tip

Make sure you let others know that you've let an employee loose on a job. Then they won't question her authority.

Some form of follow-up can be reassuring for workers who lack confidence or have some nagging doubts after you've handed down the work. It may be important to let them know that this isn't a do-or-die proposition, and they aren't being cast adrift. You may want the reassurance of periodic contact as well, of course, because you have a major stake in your employee's success.

I've had the good fortune to work for several outstanding delegators, but they always stressed the need for me to keep them informed with comments like "Keep me posted," "I don't like surprises," and "If you run into trouble, get me in the boat with you."

As part of your discussion about follow-up, clarify what results you expect and how the worker's progress will be measured. Use quantified measuring devices whenever possible. These might include, for example, reports that summarize changes in dollars or percentages since the last work period or the total number of cases processed or problems resolved during the previous week or month.

The objectivity of such measures leaves little or no debate about how well your employee is doing. Identify and agree on deadlines, key checkpoints, and major milestones.

Get the Word Out

Meeting with your delegate is only one side of the communication coin. You should also inform the necessary third parties in your own company and suppliers' and customers' organizations and ask them to contact your employee on delegated issues from now on. Provide relevant information about your action if appropriate, but without seeming to ask for their blessing or compromising or diluting your delegate's new status and authority.

Some colleagues inside and outside your company may get their knickers in a twist over what you've done. They may feel that their status is decreased because they won't be dealing directly with you.

If so, so be it. You may elect to give them the courtesy of an explanation, but the choice to delegate is yours, and you made it for good reason. Expect a period of griping and grumbling while you forward their communications and requests to your delegate. Eventually they'll learn the new order of things.

The Agile Manager's Checklist

✔ Before you discuss your delegation plan with an employee, consider the impact of potential language barriers, the worker's willingness to ask you questions, and the need to provide a model or visual aid.

✔ Agree on a starting date for your employee to take over the things you've delegated; allow some preparation time if necessary. Set an end date for one-time jobs.

✔ Define the limits of the employee's decision-making power and what degree of authority you intend to grant.

✔ Tell workers how you're going to follow up and what kind of progress reports, if any, they'll have to make.

✔ Secure the employee's firm commitment to do good work.

✔ Inform the appropriate people of your action and tell them to deal with your employee on the issues you've delegated.

Chapter Five

Deal with Resistance

"The style of participative management is at its best when the supervisor can draw out the best in . . . people, allow decisions to be made at the point of influence and contribution, and create a spirit that everyone is in it together and that if something is unknown, they'll learn it together."

JOSEPH A. RAELIN,
BOSTON COLLEGE SCHOOL OF MANAGEMENT

Judy tapped on Phil's cubicle door later that day. Phil invited her in. He stared closely at her for a moment; it appeared she might have been crying.

"I'm not sure I can do this job," she said.

"What's the problem?"

"I just don't think I'm ready for it," she said with a toss of her head. Phil wondered if she'd practiced that.

He felt his anger rising but subdued it. "Are you telling me the whole story?" He remained silent, a technique to get people to talk that someone had told him about.

After twenty painful seconds, she broke down. "No," she said. She paused for a few seconds, then said earnestly, "It's Will and Mike. They both started ribbing me about the job, then they turned *mean. Will said to Mike, so I could hear, 'Why are they letting someone just out of college do work like that? She ought to be doing grunt work for a few years like I did."*

"That b—" Phil caught himself just in time and counted to five silently. "You realize," he continued, "they are jealous."

"I know, but I have to work with them a lot. And I want to be on good terms with them both," she said without much conviction.

"I want you to do this job. And I know you can do it. Besides, it'll be good for your career. I'll back you up 100 percent, and so will the boss. In fact, I'll take care of those two right now—"

"Don't! Then they'll say I ran to you for protection." Realizing what was at stake, newfound resolve filled her. "I'll take care of them myself. And I'll do the job."

The movie thriller *Marathon Man* showed one dramatic technique for dealing with resistance. Sir Laurence Olivier, playing the part of a fugitive Nazi war criminal, was trying to extract information from Dustin Hoffman. He drugged him and bound him firmly to a chair. When Hoffman revived, Olivier took a high-speed dentist's drill and began drilling into the nerve of one of his front teeth without giving Hoffman the benefit of anesthetic, pausing occasionally to ask, "Is it safe?"

> **Best Tip**
>
> To employees who may feel—or be—overworked, be sure to communicate the importance of the job.

This technique for overcoming resistance would be difficult to use on your employees, of course. Do you know how to calculate the proper drug dosage for each worker on your staff? Where could you find a dental drill, unless you work in a medical center? Even if you did, some busybody would probably hear your worker's screams and blow your whole plan. And let's not even think about the trouble you'd get in for practicing dentistry without a license. So you're probably better off trying a different technique, one that's likely to be, ah, safer.

Let's start by looking at why workers resist delegation. Why would you? For the following seven reasons:

1. Lack of Confidence

Most of us hate to admit self-doubt, even to ourselves. It's even harder to bare our souls to someone else, especially a boss who senses indecision if your finger hovers too long between the Coke and Pepsi buttons on the break room soda machine.

Deep down, however, some workers may fear that they don't have the skills, training, or experience to do a job right—and they're understandably embarrassed and reluctant to say so.

2. A Feeling of Being Dumped On

"I know garbage rolls downhill, but why am I always living in the valley?" That pithy little aphorism pops up on many office bulletin boards and is often muttered into a gin and tonic or two after work.

In times of downsizing (and at other times, for that matter), workers may feel victimized by delegation. They worry that this new job, when piled on top of their present load, will be the straw that breaks the long-suffering camel's back.

One manufacturing company recently doubled its size by buying a competitor but failed to expand its customer service staff accordingly. Employees worked twelve-hour days regularly just to keep their heads above water.

In response to complaints about their plight, the president called a meeting. He reminisced about his early days as an accountant and the times he'd worked until midnight and during weekends to get important projects done on time. He closed by saying that he didn't see anyone doing that in this case, so the employees were obviously wrong about being overworked and actually had no problem.

The last chapter recommended some ways to deal with this feeling; no need to repeat them here. Let's just emphasize that if you don't communicate your assignment carefully and underscore its merit and value, your worker may feel like a fire hydrant and you're just another dog.

3. Disproportionate Pay

People have a fine-tuned sense of equity. If they believe there's a major gap between the size of their paycheck and the size and number of tasks or decisions you've laid on them, expect them to object (through words, actions, or inaction) that you're disrespecting them. Can you blame them? Pay and accountability should run hand in hand.

Battling the Budget Monster is beyond the scope of this book. Suffice it to say, however, that your fair play monitor should sound an alarm when employees' pay and authority get out of synch.

Go to bat for your people. Fight for the money you need to make adequate pay adjustments. Do that, and you'll live up to their expectations and keep your part of your moral contract with them.

4. Fear of Becoming a Scapegoat

Remember that little railroad ditty at the beginning of chapter three? If not, go back and read it again (page 33); it's certainly apropos here. Agile managers, of course, have more character than to use their employees as ducks in a shooting gallery, but many of your workers may still adopt the motto of Missouri (the "Show Me" state).

Best Tip

If people feel they are underpaid for the work you give them, expect objections. (Perhaps with good reason.)

If you've just taken charge of your group, you should invent opportunities to show them that you're above such a tacky tactic. People who are new to your group should find out from the old heads just how evenhanded you are, but they deserve proof, too. Combine your words, actions, and hard-won reputation to dispel any hint that you'd sacrifice your delegates on the altar of your own ego if they make a mistake.

This won't happen overnight. Every working day brings ways to prove yourself and confirm your dedication to ethical values.

5. 'That's Not My Job'

Sound familiar? You've probably thought or said that several times yourself during your career, and your employees are likely to do so when you lay some serious delegation on them.

Today's emphasis on customer service and cross-training requires all of us to be more flexible, team-oriented, and open to delegation than ever before. With that in mind, you can try to counter this line of resistance to delegation in several ways.

Criticize the attitude, not the person. Try comments such as:

- "Our department can't compete in today's climate unless everyone pulls together. That means making extra efforts from time to time."
- "Our competitors are broadening employees' authority, and we've got to do so as well. Cutbacks and right-sizing make cooperation a survival skill. Each of us has to understand that."
- "Lots of us feel that way now and then, but top management expects more flexibility and cross-training. We can't work with blinders on anymore."

Praise your worker's strengths. Tell the employee that he or she is your first choice for the assignment (if that's true) because of previous performance or other qualities. ("I really want *you* to tackle this, Jean. You're reliable, and you did a good job on the Owens order.") Praise boosts people's confidence and self-esteem.

Emphasize the assignment's personal benefits. One of the most effective responses to the "not my job" refrain is to say to the employee "Here's what's in it for you." Describe how the assignment will increase the worker's competence and value to the organization. New skills, flexibility, and objectivity enhance someone's potential and promotability, not to mention job security.

You can also get personal about yourself. Mention times in your career when you wisely agreed to go the extra mile for one of your bosses. Reflect on the experience, perspective, versatility, and other benefits that you gained as a result.

Take care, of course, not to sound like you're making a veiled threat. ("If you give me a hard time about this, I'll get even.") Use yourself as a positive example of how accepting an additional assignment willingly at the right time and place can pay off in the long run.

In addition, you could mention jobs you're doing now that don't seem to fall entirely within your job description. That underscores the fact that you're not asking more from your people than you are from yourself.

Emphasize the need for customer service. Customer service is everybody's job. Customers couldn't care less who's responsible for solving their problems. They want satisfaction, not foot-dragging, whining, or complaints.

Leading-edge companies, departments, managers, and employees let outstanding customer service drive everything they do. Make your workers put service first; you can sort out the details later.

Cite business conditions. Today's business setting is a compelling reason for all employees to accept assignments that may push their job's limits. Foreign and domestic competition calls for more cooperation than ever before.

Make flexibility your motto. You can short-circuit potential resistance from applicants and new hires by discussing your views about delegation—and the requirement to be flexible—during employment interviews and orientation.

If you take over a group of seasoned employees, you may want to summarize your views during your first department meeting.

In the latter case, ask the outgoing manager to assess the group's attitude about working close to the boundaries of their job descriptions and proceed accordingly.

Once you've made your initial point, confirm through individual follow-up contact and your own work habits that customer service, cooperation, and teamwork must have top priority. Setting that standard and expecting others to meet it can help your department and each of your employees to excel.

When business is tight, you can't afford to let employees be as narrow-minded as they were in boom times. Everyone has to help pick up the slack caused by layoffs and consolidated jobs and departments. Union contracts notwithstanding, job descriptions should be rewritten, with more flexible language if necessary, to reflect these realities.

6. Concern About Fair Treatment

Some reluctant delegates may feel they're being victimized by your action. If you ask people to do something above their present labor grade, arrange for higher pay to reward the greater accountability or skill.

If you draft people for work below their labor grade, emphasize that their pay won't be reduced. Rotate unpleasant work among your staff so no one feels singled out, and clarify that you're being as evenhanded as possible under the circumstances.

"Fair," of course, is a highly subjective word. Providing a rationale for an assignment and pointing out its role and benefits in the total scheme of things is sound management practice, but don't become defensive or let the discussion with your worker escalate into a debate.

Best Tip

Rewrite job descriptions when business conditions change. Everyone must be flexible to stay competitive.

Regardless of whether the employee agrees with you, you've provided the courtesy of an explanation. With few exceptions (one of which will be mentioned soon), your wishes should carry the day.

7. Co-workers' Reactions

Your delegates may also resist taking on more duties because they dread confrontations with or resentment from some colleagues. For example, they may feel ill at ease with notoriously obnoxious individuals who pointedly ignore or refuse to accept their increased authority and try to bypass them to deal directly with you. (You, of course, should be prepared to rebuff these attempts, as mentioned earlier.)

If you've delegated authority to a youthful worker, older peers may vent their bitterness with snide remarks and an uncooperative attitude. ("Sending a girl to do a woman's job," "Boss's pet," "Still wet behind the ears" "Come back when your voice changes, Junior," etc.) Other employees, as mentioned earlier, may object to the decreased status that comes with dealing through an underling.

Best Tip

Back up the authority you've granted a worker—especially to jealous co-workers, but also to those in other departments.

These experiences can be a real trial by fire for your newly anointed employee, but what manager hasn't endured them? As Ernest Hemingway said, "Life breaks all of us, but we grow stronger in the broken places."

Reinforce and confirm your worker's authority to everyone who tries to disregard or undermine it, and provide a sympathetic ear when the going gets tough. Leave no doubt, however, that you expect your worker to hang in there and get the job done.

The owner of a successful auto dealership considered the friction and jealously that accompany delegation a major rite of passage and a litmus test for all of his aspiring higher management candidates.

"If they can't cut it at this level, I don't see how I can promote them any higher," he said. "A certain amount of heckling, needling, and resentment are going to exist in any business organization. I look for people who can stand up to and rise above their envious co-workers' bitching and griping and handle the authority I've given them with class and style. Those who do get rewarded in my company, and everybody knows it."

Sound Out Misgivings and Concerns

It's often helpful to let new and uncertain delegates vent their feelings about your assignment and the changes that may be in store. Without sounding like Perry Mason, ask diagnostic questions such as:

1. *What specific parts of the work are you most uncomfortable with?*
2. *Are there any more resources that I might be able to provide? If so, what are they?*
3. *What parts of the assignment aren't clear?* (Don't hesitate to ask this question several times.)
4. *What additional training or experience would help you feel more comfortable with this job once you get under way?*
5. If the assignment will bring the employee into the orbit of several new people or departments inside or outside your company: *What would you like me to say on your behalf when I tell them that you're going to be the new contact person on this job?*

These questions help you get a fix on your employee's main concerns by revealing objections that may have been hidden until now. If nothing else, they're further evidence of your concern for and commitment to your worker's success.

A parting thought: If your first choice is absolutely dead-set against the task but is an otherwise stellar performer, try not to let the disputed assignment become the flash point that may touch off a resignation.

This isn't to say that you should allow people to threaten or negotiate their way out of unwanted jobs. After all, you're the boss.

Nevertheless, if you're convinced that mandating the assignment would force a virtually indispensable employee to resign and handicap your department's performance, a damn-the-torpedoes position could be costly. Consider another candidate if your authority and leadership won't be compromised by doing so.

Build Your Delegate's Confidence

Taking on a new assignment can be like going on a blind date. You're not sure what sort of creature you're going to be stuck with.

Here are several techniques you can use to boost your delegates' confidence and productivity while helping them come up to speed as soon as possible. The faster they do, the fewer demands they'll make on you.

Build originals, not clones. To echo the ideas in chapter three, good managers elevate results above methods. Perhaps Gen. George S. Patton said it best: "Never tell people *how* to do things. Tell them *what* to do, and they will surprise you with their ingenuity."

Realizing there can be many routes to the same destination, you can allow your people to find their own path, as long as they don't lose their bearings. The ultimate benefit? You may discover that neophytes invent ways to do things that are better than yours or "the way we've always done it here."

Delegate noncritical tasks that are challenging yet achievable. This is sound philosophy when you're using delegation primarily as a training-and-development tool. Letting new people test their wings on a series of challenging tasks where mistakes can't do too much damage is always a good idea. They experience success incrementally, and their confidence grows accordingly.

When inexperienced workers achieve goals that demonstrate growth and success, point them out. They may be standing too close to appreciate such mini-milestones for what they are.

While you're at it, contrast these examples of increased proficiency with earlier, less adept performances to underscore how the employee has progressed compared with, say, last week or last month.

Sandwich criticism between praise. When something goes haywire, try not to blow the error out of proportion. Start by praising positive accomplishments, then discuss what needs correcting and close with a note of praise. For example:

"I'm glad to see how fast you've learned to sort these invoices, Tom. The people in Accounts Payable noticed that several were misfiled, though, so I want you to take a bit more time until you have the routine down pat. Overall, you're coming along fine."

This practice lets you get your message across in a way that's not entirely negative or critical. A steady diet of criticism can make the most enthusiastic delegate gag. The criticism sandwich recognizes that good things are happening, too.

Best Tip

Delegate noncritical tasks to inexperienced workers. Succeeding in them bolsters their confidence and increases their value to you.

Express confidence in your worker's abilities. It's a real ego boost to hear someone say, "I think you can do it." Coaches have applied this technique for decades, and agile managers do, too.

Confidence is contagious. Tell your people you believe in them, and you lead them to believe in themselves. One of the greatest satisfactions of management is to ask more from your people than they believe they can do—and then help them celebrate the success when they discover they really could handle the task after all.

Acknowledge the value of previous experience. Ask delegates who have worked elsewhere to compare your systems and procedures with those of former employers. You might learn some useful techniques that you could use in your department. You never know until you ask.

Even if some workers have no meaningful experience, you can at least point out that they're contributing a unique viewpoint to the job. That's a perspective uncorrupted by rules and procedures that, if challenged by a fresh thinker, may prove to be worth overhauling.

Emphasize potential. Emphasizing potential encourages new workers to focus their energy on growth and development. When you assure workers that you're concerned with enhancing their future value—and they're not expected to become instant experts—you relieve some of the natural pressure that comes from being given a new job to do.

The Agile Manager's Checklist

✔ Understand that employees resist delegated work because of:

- A lack of confidence;
- A sense of being dumped on;
- Inadequate pay;
- Worry that they might become scapegoats;
- Belief that the work isn't within their job descriptions;
- Concern about potential conflicts with co-workers.

✔ Take time to sound out a worker who seems deeply concerned about the assignment you're delegating.

✔ Build up the confidence of employees when handing down unfamiliar tasks or decisions.

Chapter Six

Oversee the Job

"*Until we believe that the expert in any job is the person perform-ing it, we shall forever limit the potential of that person.*"

RENE MCPHERSON, FORMER CEO, DANA CORP.

"*[The best people-centered managers] model exorbitantly high standards. They demand a lot, but show by energetic example what they demand. . . . They may or may not pat people on the back often . . . [but] they do something much more important. . . . They unmistakably demonstrate belief in the talent of and concern for the dignity of each worker.*"

TOM PETERS, BUSINESS WRITER

"I'm not finding much in this area. I just thought you should know," Judy said.

"It's a minor part of the job, but I'd like you to keep at it," said Phil. "It could yield some interesting insights."

"But I've looked everywhere," said Judy testily. "I don't know if any data exist."

69

"There's information out there somewhere. I had a professor in graduate school who specialized in that sort of thing. I bet there's a listserv on the Internet that's devoted to it."

"Hmm," said Judy. "Can you find out about it and tell me how to join the news group?"

Phil pushed his glasses back up and resisted the urge to ignore her. "I've got too much going on right now. Listen: Just type in the name Seth Abjidian on a search engine and see what comes up. He was my teacher. I'll bet you'll find something."

Great, thought Judy. What support. She turned to leave.

Phil said, "Judy, wait. I really appreciate your effort. It's just that if I get into it now, then it becomes my job. And if I'm doing that job, then I'm not doing this job." He glanced down at two binders laying open on his desk. "Come back if nothing turns up. We'll try another approach."

"OK," she said with a sigh.

This is work, thought Phil.

OK, so you've decided what to delegate, evaluated your candidates, made a wise choice, communicated the assignment thoroughly, and countered any resistance. Now all you have to do is tend to your own work, right?

Not so fast.

Delegation doesn't mean abdication. Before you start patting yourself on the back, there are a few more things to consider.

Back Up Your People

It's almost certain that somebody, sometime, is going to challenge the authority of one of your workers and come whining to you. When that happens, be prepared to back your employee to the hilt.

If people who cross swords with your delegates discover they can get what they want by complaining to you, you'll undermine and demoralize them and make them look like impotent flunkies. It's one of the worst things you can do.

Defend your delegates' actions and decisions and confirm their authority. That puts others on notice that the delegation is a done deal. This reinforces your people's confidence in both themselves and you and earns their allegiance and loyalty.

This happened to me once when I disciplined an employee under authority that was delegated to me by a new supervisor whom I barely knew. In fact, she was a new hire who had worked for my company less than a week.

The employee filed a grievance. It boiled down to a my-word-against-his situation, and my new boss simply said, "I believe my managers. The action stands."

This manager continued to be

*B*est *T*ip

If you've given a delegate the authority to act, defend and confirm that authority at every turn.

my boss for several years, and I always valued the faith and trust she placed in me at a time when she herself was on uncertain ground. Support your people, and they will respect and support you.

What to Do When Delegates Bring You Problems

"We've got trouble." That announcement can make any manager's stomach churn, but it doesn't have to. Your response when this happens can have a major impact on how comfortable your delegates are communicating with you and how much initiative they use to exercise their authority without getting you involved.

Get a clear, concise summary. Ask your delegate for a synopsis of the problem. Listen carefully, then ask questions to clarify facts or gather more information. Restate what you heard to confirm that the two of you are communicating on the same wavelength.

Above all, avoid being judgmental or jumping to conclusions. It's too early for that. Your goal for the moment is to understand what has happened and why.

Phrase your questions and comments so that bad news bearers will be encouraged to express their views, elaborate on the facts, supply details, and generally volunteer more information than they otherwise would.

For example:

- "How would you describe . . ."
- "What was happening just before . . ."
- "Let me see if I understand you correctly . . ."
- "Why do you think . . ."
- "Does it make sense that . . ."
- "What else should I know that you might have overlooked?"
- "So, in your opinion, . . ."

This kind of phrasing helps to ensure a meeting of the minds. That's especially important, because you're working with secondhand information, and you need to make every effort to understand it clearly. Feel free to talk with other employees if you think additional opinions or viewpoints would help clarify the situation.

Best Tip

Get employees to sort out and summarize the problems they bring you by asking open-ended questions.

Remember, too, that people are usually nervous about bringing bad news in case the boss decides to shoot the messenger. Being calm and patient enhances your reputation as a cool head who doesn't shoot from the hip—you'll be the Clint Eastwood of agile managers. Your people will be more willing to keep you informed, because you've shown them that they won't become scapegoats for what happened or lightning rods for your wrath.

Ask for a solution. Once you've clarified the situation, ask the employee, "What do you think we should do?" Or, in certain situations, "What are you going to do?" There are two good reasons for doing this.

First, it makes workers realize that you won't allow them to dump their troubles in your lap and scurry off down the hall. If you allow such "reverse delegation" to take place, you'll be juggling so many of your employees' problems that you won't have time to handle your own. Being a sounding board, coach, advisor, and collaborator is part of your job, of course, but letting your people shift the entire burden of a problem onto your back is not.

Best Tip

Before you jump in to solve a problem, ask the employee for a solution. Say, "What do you think we should do?"

The second reason for asking for a solution is that you let your delegates know you expect them to exercise their own initiative, examine problems, and develop potential solutions before they involve you. That requirement should motivate them to think more like managers themselves, which will help them become more self-reliant, valuable, and promotable.

Assure them that you're not giving up your right to make the final decision, if you've reserved that for yourself. What you are doing, however, is establishing an informal policy that no one should bring you problems that aren't accompanied by at least one solution.

Once your people get this message, your job should be easier. Eventually, many problems that might otherwise be left on your doorstep may be solved by your people without involving you.

Let things incubate, if possible. If the course of action isn't clear or if there's a major risk riding on the outcome, don't make a snap decision. Instead,

- Take time to digest the information;
- Develop and examine alternatives with your delegate;
- Consult with colleagues or superiors;
- Ask your worker to propose additional measures that may resolve the problem.

A little incubation can do wonders for your perspective.

Delegate corrective action. Once you've decided what to do (with your delegate playing a major role when possible), let your worker implement the plan. This is especially important if your employee thought it up in the first place.

| **Best Tip**
|
| Reverse delegators sometimes throw jobs back into your lap for the mere sport of it. Don't play their game.

There's an implied vote of confidence in allowing people to put their own ideas to work. They're gratified by the knowledge that they both conceived and executed the solution. You've also made the point that you expect them to be stakeholders and collaborators—not merely messengers—when the trouble bug bites.

Provide for follow-up and feedback. If the situation calls for follow-up, assure your employees that you plan to do so, then follow through. In addition, leave your door open for feedback so they'll feel comfortable approaching you again if the solution doesn't work or if complications arise.

Guard Against 'Reverse Delegation'

Reverse delegators are birds of prey that can attack even the best managers. You have to fend them off for several key reasons.

- You can't allow delegated work to boomerang. It sends the wrong message to your workers—a message that your decisions are negotiable and easy to reverse. All they may need to do is serve you a little cheese and whine.

- You've probably filled up the new space on your calendar with other commitments. You may not have time for the delegated work even if you are willing to take it back.

- People who are allowed to reverse-delegate don't grow and may in fact handicap your growth if you're trying to "delegate yourself a promotion." Both of you may lose.

- Workers who discover they can bounce things back to you will make it a habit to do so.

But why might employees try to reverse your delegated work in the first place? Maybe because of:

- *Poor preparation.* If they believe they're improperly or insufficiently trained, they may try to slither out from under the job.
- *Fear of mistakes.* Workers who are preoccupied with the accountability end of the delegation stick may be afraid you'll wallop 'em upside the head with it when things go wrong.
- *Lack of confidence.* Highly insecure delegates who've yet to try their wings may need to be nudged out of the nest—gently, of course.
- *"CYA."* If the job doesn't work out, the worker wants to be able to say, "Hey, it's not really my fault. You said to do it that way!"
- *Discomfort with your democratic leadership style.* Employees who formerly worked for an autocratic manager who delegated little authority ("I'm paid to think; you're paid to work") may have trouble exercising the degree of discretion that you, a more participative manager, have given them. Think of it as culture shock.

Since we've classified reverse delegators as birds of prey, it helps to be able to recognize several common species. (And don't forget the first principle of bird watching: "If you're looking up, keep your mouth closed!")

Fine-feathered flatterers. These workers can't say enough great things about you, although they try. They butter you up until your cholesterol count jumps fifty points. Then, because they hold you in such high regard, honest they do, they're certain you'll be happy to jump right in and bail them out if there's trouble. Be on guard whenever they want to "Get the benefit of your opinion," "Touch base with you," or ask, "How would you approach this?"

Frustrated fledglings. These delegates, who may not be used to thinking for themselves, often perch on a pity pot while emitting a high, piercing cry: "I'm too stressed! I can't cope!" They hope you'll feel sorry for them and give them a hand.

Pileated procrastinators. These employees procrastinate with a purpose. They believe if they wait until things get critical, you'll dive in and save the day. Enhance their diet with heavy supplements of accountability.

Bewildered blunderers. Members of this species often camouflage themselves in confusion and minor mistakes. They're excellent actors, hoping that their histrionics will make you feel frustrated and/or sorry enough for them to take back the assignment and do it yourself. What you should reward, however, is not the bewildered blunderers' thespian skills but their performance on the work they've been delegated.

Deal with Reverse Delegators

If you're convinced that your delegate is capable of handling an assignment, use one of these techniques to keep delegated jobs from coming back to you.

- Review how you made the assignment. Was your delegate as prepared and qualified for the work as you originally believed? If not, what factors did you overlook or disregard that should have had more attention? Did you provide a sound model or example of the results your worker was accountable for? Did the employee have enough authority and resources to do the job?

   If you believe the assignment should continue, make any necessary adjustments in authority or resources and confirm your faith in the worker's ability, then . . .

- Emphasize that your calendar has since filled up with additional duties, and the delegated ball will stay in the employee's court.
- Obtain the worker's commitment to success once again.

- Make a list of "boilerplate" responses to workers' reverse-delegation tactics. If you lay these on habitual reverse delegators often enough, even the most determined ones should finally get the message. Here are a few to get you started:

—"I wouldn't have given you this work if I wasn't sure you could do it."

—"I want this assignment to be a learning experience for you. It's important that you stick with it. I'll support you any way I can."

—"You can't always hit a home run on your first trip to the plate. Keep trying. I'm impressed with your efforts."

—"I know you've tried hard, but maybe there's a better way. How else do you think you might tackle the job?"

—"I want you to give it your best shot. My schedule's too jammed for me to get involved right now."

What If It Doesn't Work?

Reverse delegators are relatively harmless manipulators who can be turned away with some practice and persistence. What should you do, however, if the assignment really jumps the track—that is, if your delegate falls drastically short of standards, makes serious mistakes, or becomes profoundly upset or frustrated with a newly assigned task?

When fending off and redirecting reverse delegators, get them to commit again to a successful outcome.

It's easy to overreact by taking back the job yourself or giving it to someone else. Either action may be wrong. Taking back the job denies your delegates the chance to straighten things out and redeem themselves. Transferring the job to a co-worker makes your original employee lose face as well as an opportunity to grow.

The best course is often to (1) examine your past delegating

Keep at it!

procedure and look for ways to improve it, (2) resist the urge to recall the task completely, and (3) work with the confused employee until he or she learns to do the job right.

1. Review how you made the assignment. This parallels your first response to reverse delegators. When you see ongoing signs of trouble, mentally review how you delegated the job in the first place. More specifically, did you:

- Set clear performance standards?
- Explain the "how-to's" of the job thoroughly?
- Actively solicit the employee's questions?
- Give the worker a model or example to measure performance against?
- Follow up after the task was assigned?

Although this exercise helps you troubleshoot your delegation technique (and perhaps correct some flaws), you'll have to go further to resolve the immediate problem.

2. Don't rescind authority completely. Your first urge might be to recall the job entirely and either do it yourself or assign it to someone else. Don't.

Overreacting by taking back a task immediately can devastate a delegate's ego and cause smoldering resentment because you deny your employee a chance to fix the problem and set things right. No one likes to lose face and be branded a failure in front of co-workers. Agile managers, like seasoned football coaches, don't bench rookie players because of one miscue.

|Best Tip

Take back a task only in the most dire situation. Doing otherwise could deal a nasty blow to an employee's ego.

Beyond your employee's feelings, however, you should also think about what you'd be doing to yourself. Rescinding authority at the first sign of trouble makes you look impulsive and indecisive.

In addition, your approach to the problem sets a precedent as far as other workers are concerned. They'll see your response as a model for how they might be treated under the same circumstances, and they'll react in one of two ways.

Snatching back new tasks at the first sign of trouble will prompt some employees to sidestep your efforts to delegate work. They won't want to be treated as incompetents if they, too, have trouble doing a new job correctly.

Best Tip

When redirecting a job, consider whether training, more authority, or more resources might ensure success.

Let them take care of it

Other workers may be prone to do a careless job, knowing that you'll shift the burden back onto your own shoulders. As one employee put it, "Why should I worry about screwing up? The first time something goes wrong, my boss will jump in with both feet and do it himself!"

3. Work with the employee. So what to do? Four steps can help to get your delegation train back on track while avoiding further trouble down the line.

Step 1: Talk before you act. Review performance standards with your delegate and explain why the work isn't acceptable. Be specific. Avoid vague remarks like, "Things aren't working out" or "I think I'd better reconsider what I gave you to do last week." People are typically hungry for details when their pride and performance are at stake. They won't be satisfied with generalities. Would you?

This conference also gives you an opportunity to establish a sense of obligation and joint commitment. After all, both of you have a vested interest in seeing that the job is done correctly.

Ask the employee to propose actions that would resolve the problem, while tactfully suggesting that more training, preparation, or authority might be in order. If the person feels ill-equipped to do the task because of one of those factors, you've made it easier to say so. Without some encouragement, people are embarrassed to admit that they're treading water.

This is also an ideal time to review the "how-to's" of the job once again. Recap your original instructions carefully (avoid remarks like "This is self-explanatory") and welcome the employee's questions by asking open-ended questions of your own that presume you haven't explained everything clearly. For example:

- "What else should we go over?"
- "Which part of the job do we need to talk about some more?"
- "What activities do you feel unclear about?"

If the delegated job has a tangible result that can be demonstrated (such as a properly formatted report or a specific production routine), set up an example that the employee can use as a model. This may be all that's necessary to eliminate confusion.

If the job consists of a central task and several satellite tasks, your worker's comments during this meeting might suggest that you take back some of the lesser ones temporarily. Doing so would give the person more time to master the core task without getting lost in details.

Best Tip

If a job in trouble has a number of tasks, consider taking back a few to help the employee focus on the rest.

When saddled with a major responsibility and a host of secondary tasks, some people panic before they get their arms around it all. "I simply couldn't juggle all the new details at once," one frustrated worker confessed. "I felt like I was trying to nail Jell-O to a tree."

Step 2: Get closure on this conference. Wrap it up with a mutually clear summary of which parts of the job, if any, you'll take back and which ones will be left with your subordinate. In addition, make sure the two of you agree on the standards that must be met, and establish a timetable for following up on progress.

This timetable is especially important. It keeps lines of communication open, provides a built-in excuse for making future contact, and assures the person that he or she isn't being left to sink or swim.

This conference and its resulting closure speak well for you. You come across as a cool-headed coach and counselor instead of an impulsive dictator or a whip-cracking galley master. Your delegate knows what's wrong and why and has an action list and perhaps a model to follow to bring the work up to standard by a specific deadline.

Step 3: Back up your words with action. Monitor your employee's performance regularly, realizing that he or she may be anxious or defensive because of the circumstances. Show concern without oversupervising, and follow up with open-ended requests or questions such as, "Tell me how everything is going," and "Which problems should we discuss?"

Make an effort to praise improvement whenever praise is justified. Praise alleviates anxiety and confirms that the person is making progress.

Step 4: Delegate additional parts of the job as performance improves. Any satellite duties that you took back in Step 1 can be redelegated as performance improves and the person gains confidence. Consider relaying these tasks piecemeal, however, so your employee can integrate them into the existing routine gradually. Passing them down all at once may trigger another round of confusion and frustration.

When you add a new segment of the job, make certain to explain its importance and emphasize how it relates to the work previously assigned. This technique helps the employee see the overall task both as a whole and as the sum of its parts—to see the forest as well as the trees.

Delegation: An Acquired Skill

Good managers realize that delegation is an acquired skill. Relaying work to subordinates successfully takes practice and the willingness to work with people who may have trouble handling an entire job all at once.

Managers who are willing to help their people over some early rough spots build a working bond that ensures that they, their delegates, and the entire organization grow beyond yesterday's skills to master the challenges of tomorrow.

The Agile Manager's Checklist

✔ Back up and confirm your employees' authority when it is challenged.

✔ Put your delegates at ease when they tell you there's trouble. Be a coach, constructive critic, and sounding board.

✔ Don't let employees dump delegated assignments back on you. Understand their reasons for doing so, but don't allow yourself to be manipulated by capable workers.

✔ Review assignments gone wrong and proceed with care. Remember: Work can be delegated by degrees as well as all at once.

Chapter Seven

Handle a Non-Delegating Boss

"Authority intoxicates."

SAMUEL BUTLER, ENGLISH POET

"Rather than allowing [delegates] the autonomy to get involved and do the work in their own ways, what happens all too often is the manager wants the workers to do it the manager's way."

EDWARD L. DECI, UNIVERSITY OF ROCHESTER

The Agile Manager caught up with Phil in the hallway. "That was a great report Judy did, Phil."

"You're telling me," said Phil. "I see at least three new product opportunities in it. And you know something—you were right. I wouldn't have done the project the way she did, and I ended up learning a lot as a result."

"That's how it's supposed to work," said the Agile Manager. "Plus you develop her skills and make her more useful."

Phil saw an opening. "Boss, you know how you have that Wednesday committee meeting that keeps you from going to the monthly marketing meeting?"

"Yeah—and it's too bad, because those meetings are important."

"I was thinking maybe I could go for you. I could bring up things you want to know about, and then give you a complete rundown later in the day."

"Thanks Phil, but I already get the minutes. Besides, it often deals with things that don't concern your job."

"I know that. I just think somebody should represent this department. Besides, I think it would make me a better product developer if I could hear the marketing side more." And, he thought, it would make me more visible within the company.

"Phil, I don't really think—" The Agile Manager stopped abruptly when his inner voice spoke up loud and clear: Non-delegators don't go far. You could make him more useful. *"Of course you can go to those meetings. That'd be a big help to me."*

Phil beamed.

Ever wonder why your boss doesn't like to delegate? Of course not—you read the all-time favorite reasons in chapter one! And while unambitious subordinates may be content to follow a set routine, like gerbils on a treadmill, both they and their gerbil soul mates will probably go nowhere fast.

Agile managers, on the other hand, want their bosses to delegate meaningful work. It's a ticket to bigger and better things: promotions, enhanced job security, and greater job satisfaction, to name a few.

Let's explore some ways to identify significant tasks or decisions that you want your boss to delegate to you, then look at ways to counteract his or her opposition to doing so.

Learn Your Boss's Job

Learning the boss's job doesn't necessarily mean learn how to do it. It means learn what it consists of. The better you understand what your boss does, the better equipped you are to identify activities that you'd benefit from doing. For example, ask yourself:

- How heavy is my boss's present workload?

- What additional assignments are pending that will make that work load even heavier?
- What tasks and decisions waste most of my boss's time? Why?
- Where are these activities ranked on my boss's priority list?
- Which activities are forcing my boss to put in the most overtime?
- Which duties does my boss usually complain about doing?
- What specific tasks that my boss does now do I think I can do better or faster? Why?
- Which tasks am I actually better qualified to do? (Although you're far too agile—let alone modest—to announce this!)

Remember, too, that some of your boss's low-priority items may be work that you could handle with ease and eventually use to showcase your own talents and ability. Agile managers are always looking for ways to manufacture career opportunities and cast their own stepping stones.

Once you've answered the above diagnostic questions, build a "hit list" of the most mutually beneficial tasks and decisions your boss could delegate. This is work that your boss would be relieved to get rid of *and* work that you can learn a lot from if it were given to you.

List these items on paper and build a strong case for your boss's delegating each of them to you. It should go without saying, of course, that you should choose your targets based on their potential for meaningful experience and approach them carefully.

Best Tip

To find opportunities to grow and learn, find out what your boss does—and where he or she could use help.

Never volunteer for marginal, menial, or dead-end work. Make certain the tasks you propose to take over complement and benefit your skills, responsibilities, and visibility within your area. Be extremely selective.

And be discreet. If you go charging up to your boss's desk, papers in hand, gesticulating wildly, he or she is likely to call security and hide under the desk. You'll seem too calculating and obvious, not to mention threatening and deranged.

Advance Your Plan

Once you've developed a wish list of work that can simultaneously advance your career and make your boss's life easier, it's time to work up some defenses in case your boss trots out (or hides behind) several of those reasons for not delegating that you read about in chapter one.

Only your boss can do it (Lone Ranger). Invent opportunities to demonstrate that you have the skills and experience that the assignments require.

Don't expect your overworked non-delegating boss to recognize these merits or make the connection on her own, however. Spell out the relationship between your qualifications and the nature of the tasks you're angling for. Promote yourself as a conscientious delegate who deserves a shot. Emphasize that there's minimal downside risk.

Fear that you'll make mistakes. Without sounding too much like an equal, adopt a "we" orientation in everything you say and do. "*Our* department," "*our* challenge," "*our* main concerns," "when *we* wrap up this project," "when *we're* finally seated on the board of directors" . . . well, you get the point.

This assures your boss that you approach your job and any delegated assignments with both of your interests and reputations in mind and will not jeopardize them in any way, shape, or form.

It may not hurt to speak the obvious: "I know that if I blow this assignment you'll hesitate to give me more meaningful work, so I pledge to do the best possible job. I'll do everything in my power not to disappoint either of us."

The more concerned and committed you are about doing a good job, the more trustworthy you'll seem. Cast yourself as a partner in your boss's success, not a bit player or a walk-on.

There's no time to teach you. If your boss believes this, make the time to teach yourself! Take the initiative to research the work you want to be involved with and become an expert.

Learn all you can by reading internal documents, researching the history of the work, attending seminars or courses to cultivate the necessary skills, and talking with others both inside and outside your organization who have experience with the job and are willing to share it with you.

Do everything possible to minimize the amount of time your boss imagines he'll have to spend training you. One of the best ways to demonstrate your motivation and concern for his time is to show that you've gone to considerable effort to qualify yourself for the assignment.

Your ambition seems threatening. A paranoid or job-scared non-delegator will get spooked if you come across as an administrative juggernaut. It's like one of those overwhelmingly energetic,

Best Tip

If the boss doesn't have the time to teach you how to do a job, teach yourself or take a class or seminar.

emotionally exhausting, enthusiastic, exuberant waiters in trendy restaurants. ("Hi! My name's Karen/Kent! I guarantee that your dining experience tonight will eclipse anything else that will happen to you in your entire lives! I love you! I want you to adopt me! Your wish is my command!")

This puts people off and raises their guard. Better to build a quiet, rock-solid case for the time you can save your boss by taking over this job and declare your commitment to doing it well.

Your boss hates to lose credit. The teamwork/partnership attitude mentioned earlier can also alleviate this motive for your boss's refusal to delegate. Your words and actions should confirm that you're not trying to hog the spotlight.

But be realistic. A flat-out paranoid, egotistical, control-freak manager can be a formidable roadblock to your growth and development. You may discover that a "lateral promotion" to another department or division may be the most practical way to get around such a person. (Where does an elephant sit? Anywhere he wants to.)

Meanwhile, if you're working for a dyed-in-the-wool credit thief, you need to ensure that you're recognized for your achievements and stand outside your boss's shadow. For example:

- Make sure your name appears on all significant proposals, memos, letters, e-mail, and other communications to confirm your contributions to major projects and decisions. Some assertive managers even send unsolicited copies to senior managers without getting their boss's approval so the higher-ups know about their involvement. While such a move may be risky, sometimes it's easier to beg forgiveness than to ask permission.

- If you work for a computer illiterate boss who thinks a hard drive is a grueling trip by automobile, you have an enormous edge when it comes to advancing your skills, reputation, and value to your company. By mastering high-profile programs and becoming a gatekeeper of the information they produce, some agile managers have actually turned the tables, making their bosses highly dependent on them.

One such manager noticed that his boss, who had minimal computer skills, consistently took credit for the proposals he labored long and hard to write by having a secretary reprint them with his name deleted.

Best Tip

Put your name on anything significant—reports, projects—that you took part in.

When several higher managers began requesting copies on disk, he knew how to get the credit he'd been denied. He filled the disk copies full of nonprinting comments, notes, and suggestions to his boss. When the higher executives called up the disk files, they instantly saw who was responsible for the work. Soon they were calling him directly with questions and bypassing his boss. Eventually he got the recognition—and the promotion—he deserved.

The Agile Manager's Legacy

Agile managers, who are consummate delegators, leave a legacy of excellence for their people and their companies. They are the quintessential "Old Tom."

"Old Tom" was a stray cat who took up residence under a storage shed in my neighbor's back yard. He sired so many off-spring that our neighborhood association took up a collection to have him neutered. After he came back, the kitten population increased even more.

"What could be causing this?" some residents wondered. "It should be obvious," I said. "Old Tom was an expert in his field—a feline agile manager. Now he's delegating all the work to the young toms."

See you later, delegator.

The Agile Manager's Checklist

✔ Learn all you can about your boss's workload, pending assignments, time-consuming tasks and decisions, and priorities.

✔ Build a list of the most mutually beneficial assignments that your boss could delegate.

✔ When you make your pitch, be prepared to rebut several common reasons that your boss may have for refusing to delegate.

✔ If you work for a boss who habitually hogs all the credit and cuts you out of the action, make sure that you receive recognition for the work you've contributed to. (Using all your political wiles, of course.)

Appendix

Internet Resources

My favorite multi-search search engine: *www.dogpile.com*. Dogpile searches:

The Web: Yahoo!, Lycos' A2Z, Excite Guide, Go2.com, PlanetSearch, Thunderstone, What U Seek, Magellan, Lycos, WebCrawler, InfoSeek, AltaVista, Excite & HotBot.

Usenet: Hotbot, Reference, Dejanews, AltaVista and Dejanews's old Database.

FTP: Filez and FTP Search.

News Wires: Yahoo News Headlines, Excite News and Infoseek NewsWires.

Users can customize Dogpile to search their favorite search engines in a specific order and bookmark the customized version for future use.

Internet Resources—Delegation

Tips on coping with a boss who doesn't delegate: *www.hardatwork.com/Stump/MTB/Delegate.html*

General suggestions for delegating work: *www.mindtools.com/ tmdelegt.html*

Top 10 secrets of safe, effective delegating: *www.topten.org/content/tt.AE3.htm*

Internet Resources—General Information

Smart Business Supersite: *smartbiz.com*

Links to government agencies: *www.whitehouse.gov/WH/html/handbook.html*

U.S. Census Bureau home page: *www.census.gov*

The Federal Web Locator: *www.law.vill.edu/Fed-Agency/fedwebloc.html*

American Management Association: *www.amanet.org*

A Business Researcher's Interests: *www.brint.com/interest.html*

Research It! Your One-Stop Reference Desk: *www.itools.com/research-it/research-it.html*

A List of Virtual Libraries on the Web: *vlib.stanford.edu/Overview.html*

Employee Relations Web Picks: *www.nyper.com*

Business Resource Center: *www.morebusiness.com*

The Ultimate Directory: *www.infospace.com*

Switchboard (Person/Company telephone directory): *www.switchboard.com*

The Electric Law Library: *www.lectlaw.com*

Quotations: *www.yahoo.com/Reference/Quotations*

Index

Assignments: communicating 46–55; explaining, 40–41; form for delegating, 52

Authority: confirming 70–71; delegating proper, 42–43; form for delegating, 52; set level of, 50–53

Basics of delegation, 34–44

Bosses: attitude toward delegating, 27–28; handling non-delegating, 84–89

Carlzon, Jan, 35

Co-workers reactions: and resistance to delegation, 64–65

Commitment: gaining employee's, 53–54

Communicating assignments, 46–55

Deadlines, 53; and delegation, 36

Decisions: delegating, 29–30

Defending employees, 70–71

Delegate: why managers don't, 10–11, 16–19

Delegating: and succession planning, 20–21; authority, 42–43, 50–53; boss's attitude toward, 27–28; clear directions, 47–49; explaining a job's value, 40–41; kinds of jobs to hand off, 30–31; programmed tasks, 30–31; reasons managers avoid, 10–11; tasks or decisions, 29–30; to the best person, 35–37; to the proper level, 35

Delegation: and career development 21; and "credit hogs," 18–19; and deadlines, 36, 53; and employee development, 40–41;

Delegation *(continued)*:
and empowerment, 21–22; and
gauging employee skills, 28–29;
and manager's tenure, 29; and
mistakes, 44; and motivation,
22; and near-fatal problems, 77–
81; and overloaded employees,
18, 59–60; and overseeing the
job, 70–82; and problems, 71–
74; and reduced turnover, 22;
and responsibility, 12–13; and
supplying resources, 43; and
teams, 11–12; basics of, 34–44;
building a hit list of jobs, 31–32;
building confidence of employees,
66–68; communicating assignments , 46–55; defining limits of,
49–50; employees reversing, 74–
77; focusing on results, 38–40;
follow-up and reporting, 54–55;
gaining commitment to, 53–54;
keeping jobs intact, 37–38;
overview of, 13–14; quiz, 23–
24; reasons employees resist, 59–
65; reasons to, 19–22; resistance
to, 58–68; roadblock to, 13;
steps to successful, 31–32; what
to hand off, 27–32
Delegators: effective 39; no natural,
9
Directions: providing clear, 47–49

Employee development, 40–41
Employees: and mistakes, 44; and
problems, 71–74; building
confidence of, 66–68; choosing
for a job, 35–37; encouraging
them to accept assignments, 61–
63; expressing confidence in, 67;
gauging skills, 28–29; helping

get back on track, 77–81;
meeting agenda with, 46–53;
providing directions to, 47–49;
sounding out misgivings about
delegation, 65–66; who resist
delegation, 58–68; who reverse
delegate, 74–77

Fair treatment: and resistance to
delegation, 63–64
Follow-up, 54–55

Jobs: keeping intact, 37–38
Jobs to hand off, 30–31

Learn your boss's job, 84–86
Limits: defining, 49–50

Managers: and responsibility, 12–13,
17; and why they don't delegate,
10–11, 16–19; reasons to
delegate, 19–22
Managing: delegation quiz, 23–24;
explaining reasons for delegating
to self, 34; fending off reverse
delegators, 74; handling a non-
delegating boss, 84–89; overseeing a job, 70–82
Meeting with employees, 46–53
Meetings: reasons for formal, 46–47
Mistakes: and delegation, 44
Motivating: through delegation, 22

Non-delegating bosses: handling,
84–89

Overseeing the delegated job,
70–82

Pay: and resistance to delegation, 60

Plain language: using, 48
Problems: dealing with, 71–74; diagnosing, 71–74; near fatal, 77–81
Proper level: delegating to, 35

Quiz on delegating, 23–24

Reasons employees resist delegation, 59–65
Reasons to delegate, 19–22
Reporting, 54–55
Resistance: dealing with, 58–68
Resources: rounding up, 43
Results: focusing on, 38–40
Results Group, the, 51–52
Results Group's delegating form, 52
Reverse delegation, 74–77; how to

deal with, 76–77
Solutions: a methodology for gaining, 71–74; when delegation isn't working, 77–81
Steps to successful delegation, 31–32
Subordinates. *See* Employees
Succession planning: and delegating, 20–21

Tasks: delegating, 29–30
Team delegation, 11–12
Tenure on the job, 29
Turnover: and delegation, 22

Work: reasons to delegate, 19–22
Workload: and resistance to delegation, 59–60